# DON'T LET THEM BURY MY STORY

# DON'T LET THEM BURY MY STORY

## The Oldest Living Survivor of the Tulsa Race Massacre in Her Own Words

VIOLA FORD FLETCHER

WITH HER GRANDSON IKE HOWARD

Don't Let Them Bury My Story:
The Oldest Living Survivor of the Tulsa Race Massacre
in Her Own Words
by Viola Ford Fletcher & Ike Howard

BIO002010 BIOGRAPHY & AUTOBIOGRAPHY / Cultural, Ethnic & Regional / African American & Black
HIS056000 HISTORY / African American & Black
BIO026000 BIOGRAPHY & AUTOBIOGRAPHY / Personal Memoirs
978-1-737168-40-9 (Hardcover)
978-1-7371684-1-6 (Ebook)

Interior Photo Credits:
Viola Ford Fletcher Foundation and
Tulsa Historical Society & Museum

Printed in the United States of America

Mocha Media Publishing
2600 Adam Clayton Powell Boulevard
New York, NY 10039

*To the individuals and families whose lives were forever changed that day.*

# A Note From Mother Fletcher

Please help me make the world a better
place by recognizing my foundation at
**www.violafordfletcherfoundation.org**.

We serve the people of Africa in areas
of population health. After all, everyone deserves
to live a long, healthy, peaceful life!

# Contents

# Publisher's Note
## Mocha Ochoa

Mary Prince, an enslaved woman born in Bermuda in 1788, made history in 1831 as the first Black Woman to write her life story as a form of resistance against slavery. Her autobiography *The History of Mary Prince* became popular in London and an important reference for the Parliament of the United Kingdom as they considered whether or not to abolish slavery. As the years passed, Prince's book has been lost to history, rarely mentioned among other narratives by enslaved individuals or other moment-defining books. Nevertheless, her decision to write her story gave it value, and still today, it offers an important glimpse inside a wretched institution and its human toll.

In 1848, Fredrick Douglass asked the readers of his newspaper, *The North Star*, "How can we improve the lives of African Americans?" In a letter, then twenty-five-year-old Mary Ann Shadd answered with a demand. She wrote, "We should do more and talk less." She was tired of the rhetoric and empty promises by the leaders of the day. She wanted to see progress. Douglas published her letter, thus launching her career as a prominent literary activist. Shadd knew that important Black voices in Canada and the United States were suppressed and deserved a wider audience. So she acted and founded *The Provincial Freeman*, a newspaper promoting antislavery, temperance, and literature.

The Nardal Sisters – Paulette, Jane, and Andree – established a literary gathering in 1920s Paris, creating a space for writers of the African Diaspora to discuss global liberation. Their weekly meetings attracted the likes of James Baldwin, Langston Hughes, Josephine Baker, and Marcus Garvey. From these discussions, the sisters gleaned enough information to establish two newspapers that promoted a global race consciousness and called for equality and recognition of Black humanity. With an international network, they created a worldwide distribution model that facilitated the establishment and rapid growth of the literary resistance movement known as Négritude. They knew a Diasporan platform was needed to promote the global liberation of Black people, so they built it.

The Kitchen Table: Women of Color Press was established in 1981 by Barbara Smith, Audre Lorde, Cherríe Moraga, and Hattie Gossett. This publication promoted the works of Black women and was the first independent publisher dedicated to publishing literature by women of color. They knew space was needed to amplify the voices of those who were often marginalized. So, they built it.

Over the past five years, I've unearthed numerous stories while researching for Mocha Media Publishing, stories of historical significance to Black people worldwide. I've encountered hidden figures who have greatly influenced our people's trajectory but were never acknowledged, celebrated, and sometimes erased from history altogether. This is a travesty and it stems from systems that have kept people of African descent from setting the standards for which their works are judged.

Just consider the way our culture, stories, and legacies are being erased or undervalued in front of our faces. Critical race theory, the study of racism's impact, has become a target for conservative activists in the US who feel threatened by our truth. In some states, our stories now have to pass a litmus test of importance or relevance; It no longer matters whether or not it is a historical fact. Our work is validated by nods, awards, checks, and social media likes that aren't rooted in our experience or the standards we set. But let's suppose that they were. Because no one deserves to have their work judged by those who do not have the capacity or desire to fully understand its significance.

In 2021, I relocated to New York with the goal of building out a publishing enterprise. The following year, in 2022, I received Viola Ford Fletcher's manuscript. Despite a year of reaching out and attending meetings, I became dismayed when I was unable to find a partner to help publish Mother Fletcher's story. This experience is indicative of the genuine disappointment that I and other Black and Brown colleagues face in the publishing world. We rarely decide how our stories are deemed worthy, which should receive minimal support or all the bells and whistles. But, as Mary Prince, Mary Ann Shadd, the Nardal Sisters, Barbara Smith and the others have shown us, we can act.

Synchronicities are fascinating, As fate would have it, I found a way to publish the book. After a conversation with Jamol Pugh, founder of 4Black Wall Street, we decided to form a partnership and combine resources with expertise to bring *Don't Let Them Bury My Story!* to the world without apology or conforming to some arbitrary literary standard. I am grateful beyond measure to have a partner whose goals align with mine and who knows the values of our stories.

Mocha Media Publishing is committed to capturing the voices of those like Mother Fletcher who inspire us and whose stories remind us of our implicit worth. It will provide a platform for authors and thought leaders to publish content that encourages discussion, spawns ideas and movements, offers solutions, and improves the Black experience through empowerment and liberation.

My favorite writer and activist the late, Suzanne Cesaire knew how art, spirituality, and resistance were interconnected. She called it "Afro-surrealism." Cesaire believed that Afro-surrealism had the power to awaken the most disadvantaged and inspire a revolutionary attitude toward life. I believe we have all witnessed the essence of this idea through the life of Mother Fletcher. She tapped into her magic and found power in its depths. My prayer is that Mocha Media Publishing . . . and you can continue to do the same.

CATALOG #A2466, COLLECTION: Tulsa Race Massacre,
OBJECT: Negative, Sheet Film, DATE: 6/1/1921

# Foreword

## Hughes "Uncle Redd" Van Ellis

## A NOTE ON THE FOREWORD

On May 19, 2021, Hughes Van Ellis, also known as Uncle Redd, testified alongside his older sister Viola Ford Fletcher and their fellow survivor, Mother Randle, before the US Congressional Subcommittee on the Constitution, Civil Rights, and Civil Liberties. At 101 years old, Redd is one of the last remaining survivors of the Tulsa Race Massacre of 1921, an act of terror that destroyed Greenwood, Oklahoma, and many Black lives. Despite the hardships he faced, including racial segregation and discrimination, Redd remains a firm believer in the ideals of America and the promise of "liberty and justice for all."

*Chair Cohen, Ranking Member Johnson, and members of the subcommittee, my name is Hughes Van Ellis, and I am 100 years old. I am a survivor of the Tulsa Race Massacre.*

*Because of the massacre, my family was driven out of our home. We were left with nothing. We were made refugees in our own country.*

*My childhood was hard, and we didn't have much. We worried what little we had would be stolen from us, just like it was stolen in Tulsa. You may have been taught that when something is stolen from you, you can go to the courts to be made whole; you can go to the courts to get justice. This wasn't the case for us.*

*The courts in Oklahoma wouldn't hear us. The Federal courts said we were too late. We were made to feel that our struggles were unworthy of justice; that we were less valued than Whites; that we weren't fully Americans.*

*We were shown that in the United States not all men were equal under the law. We were shown that, when Black voices called out for justice, no one cared.*

*We still had faith things would get better. We still believed in the promise of America and in the cause of freedom.*

*I did my duty in World War II. I served in combat in the Far East with the 234th AAA Gun Battalion. We were an all-Black battalion. I fought for freedom abroad, even though it was ripped away from me at home, even after my home and my community were destroyed. It is because I believed, in the end, America would get it right.*

*When I returned home from the war, I didn't find any of this freedom I was fighting for overseas. Unlike White servicemen, I wasn't entitled to GI bill benefits because of the color of my skin. I came home to segregation, a separate and unequal America. Still, I believed in America.*

*This is why we are still speaking up today, even at this age of 100. The Tulsa Race Massacre isn't a footnote in the history book for us. We live with it every day, and the thought of what Greenwood was and what it could have been.*

*We aren't just Black and White pictures on a screen; we are flesh and blood. I was there when it happened; I am still here.*

*My sister was there when it happened; she is still here.*

*We are not asking for a handout. All we are asking for is for a chance to be treated like a first-class citizen who truly is a beneficiary of the promise that this is a land where there is "liberty and justice for all."*

*We are asking for justice for a lifetime of ongoing harm that was caused by the massacre. You can give us the chance to be heard and give us a chance to be made whole after all these years and after all our struggle.*

*I still believe in America. I still believe in the ideals that I fought overseas to defend. I believe, if given this chance, you will do the right thing and justice will be served. Please do not let me leave this earth without justice, like all the other massacre survivors.*

*I want to say I appreciate being here, and I hope we all will work together. We are one.*

*We are one.*

Hughes "Uncle Redd" Van Ellis

# Introduction

Ike Howard, grandson of Viola Ford
Fletcher

Memory is an indelible and important part of human social culture. We build families and civilizations based on two things: memory and vision; a vision of the future and the kinds of things we want for our children, our descendants, and how they will remember us.

Like many of her generation, born just after the turn of the century from the 1800s to the 1900s, my paternal grandmother, Viola Ford Fletcher (age 108 at the time of this writing) has a deep well of memories from which to draw, especially those related to her many childhood friends, family members like her mother, father, her siblings, the Greenwood community, and the terrible events that resulted in the obliteration of the world that she knew and thought would always be there. The story that unfolds in the following pages represents a lifetime of memories that have haunted my paternal grandmother, Viola Ford Fletcher, for the last 100 years.

By 1921, Tulsa's Greenwood district had become a prosperous, family-oriented, autonomous Black community of more than 10,000 people. In its time, Greenwood was known as one of the wealthiest Black communities in the state of Oklahoma, and possibly in the United States of America itself. This was quite a legacy of achievement for a people who had risen up from chattel slavery and centuries of racial oppression. Greenwood was also known as a place where Black folks migrating across the country from the South could find a home-cooked meal and rent a room for a few nights before moving westward.

Many Black Oklahomans legitimately claim Native American blood and tribal connections. Our family is no exception. Land given to Freedmen by their former Native American masters, though poor in its agricultural value, was found to contain petroleum oil. The Oklahoma Oil Boom of the 1900s generated much of Greenwood's Black wealth. One of the richest benefactors of the Oklahoma oil boom was Sarah Rector, a young Muskogee-Creek colored girl who was hailed by W.E.B. Dubois and Booker T. Washington as the richest young woman of those times. Other Blacks, like Sarah Rector, who were considered second-class citizens and who were now freed slaves, were doing economically better than the average White man in the City of Tulsa . . . for a time.

The Tulsa Race Massacre was like a bad dream, one that you wake up from, but find out that it happened in real life. On May 31, 1921, an enraged mob descended on the Greenwood district of the City of Tulsa, Oklahoma, for two days and burned the most prosperous Black community in the United States to the ground. Black families, including my great-grandparents Lucinda and

John, had to escape the horrific violence and destruction with just what they could carry.

On the first night of the massacre, over 2,000 individuals, including members of the Ku Klux Klan descended on Greenwood, armed to the teeth and motivated by vengeance. My grandmother, Viola Ford Fletcher, vividly recalls the terror of that night and how she, along with her parents, great-uncles, and great-aunts, made their escape. "My parents did all they could just to calm us," she told me. "But it was no use. We saw everything. The fire. The violence. The railroad tracks leading out of Tulsa were flooded with people crying and screaming." To this day, the road and railroad tracks serve as a chilling reminder of the horror my family experienced.

Jim Crow, a system of laws designed to enforce racial segregation ruled, and the prevailing "White is right," coupled with the lack of moral integrity of so-called "Bible Belt" Americans contributed to the events that led to the destruction and the violent dispersal of friends and neighbors, their escape and exile to the wilderness and into poverty. Some White citizens of Greenwood were deputized by the local government – armed to the teeth, and seeking "justice" based on a lie. Their actions created a public nuisance and psychological trauma that persists to this very day.

In 1919, just two years before the Tulsa Massacre, Black Americans were subject to a horrific display of racial terror that is historically remembered as The Red Summer–'red' being the color of blood. That unfortunate summer, scores of Black towns and townships were attacked by the Ku Klux Klan and other so-called White Supremacists. Across America, Blacks were lynched, murdered, and even burned to death alive by mobs. Stories circulated of Black army veterans, returning home from France where they fought in World War I, who were castrated and then had their genitals placed in their mouths. The Red Summer, culminating in 1921 with the Tulsa Massacre, represented a disgraceful moment in America's history. But why?

Less than a decade after slavery ended in 1865, Blacks built autonomous communities, founded successful businesses, and even a banking system. On their own, the Black communities were growing and thriving. The success of Greenwood earned it the nickname "Black Wall Street." Evidence presented in the aftermath of the Red Summer and Tulsa Massacre revealed that they were the result of White's deeply-rooted hatred of Black prosperity.

The historical economics of financial money multipliers applied to Black Wall Street estimate that the "Black Dollar" circulated within Greenwood more than thirty times over an entire year before leaving the community. This fact is crucial in understanding the root cause of the Black Wall Street Massacre, which was fueled by white supremacy, jealousy, and hate against a community considered to be populated by second-class citizens and descendants of slaves.

The human toll of the event was immense. Survivors of the massacre and their descendants estimate that far more than 300 people were killed, possibly as many as 3,000, many of whom are believed to have been buried in mass graves, or were thrown into the river, or perished in homes and businesses burned beyond recognition, nameless and un-mourned. Those who escaped would suffer from post-traumatic stress syndrome (PTSD) and generational trauma.

The economic and financial toll was substantial. For Greenwood's Black communities, damages from the massacre included the loss of 600 businesses, 21 churches, 21 restaurants, 30 grocery stores, 2 movie theaters, 6 private airplanes, a hospital, a bank, a post office, schools, libraries, law offices, and Greenwood's private bus system. Some estimated the amount to be $1.5 million in real estate, which, in today's currency, would be valued at over $47.6 million. However, experts and researchers advocating for reparations argue that these estimates fall significantly short of the actual value of damages. For them, the value is estimated at more like $30 million in 1921 dollars, which equates to nearly $60 billion in 2023.

Because of the staggering human and economic toll resulting from the massacre, the city of Tulsa continues to grapple with its past. It remains haunted by this dark chapter, especially considering the context of emerging and accurately rewritten American history. A stark reminder of Tulsa's troubled past can be found in a street called "Reconciliation Way," which was originally named after Tate Brady, one of the city's founders who had ties to the Ku Klux Klan and the massacre.

In response to public pressure, Tulsa's city council changed the name to honor Mathew Brady, a renowned Civil War photographer with no known connection to Tulsa. However, many critics, particularly in the African American community, found this so-called compromise to be unsatisfactory, dismissing it as a mere smokescreen. The name was then changed to the hopeful-sounding "Reconciliation Way," which implies the restoration of friendly relations after a period of conflict. This could not be further from the truth for the survivors of the massacre.

For many in Tulsa's African American community, the name change to "Reconciliation Way" was seen as a superficial attempt to brush over the deep-seated wounds and injustices inflicted upon victims of the massacre. It was viewed as a hollow gesture that failed to address the systemic racism, violence, and economic destruction that occurred in Greenwood, and the continued impact it has on generations of Black Tulsans.

The name change did little to acknowledge the true history of the area and the need for genuine reconciliation and accountability for the atrocities that were committed. It was seen by many as a mere cosmetic change that did not address the root causes of the racial disparities that persist in the city to this day.

Reconciliation is a noble concept, but the real question that begs an answer is, "Where is justice?" When will it finally be served? As the oldest living survivor of the massacre, my paternal grandmother, along with the two other remaining survivors, her brother, Mr. Hughes Van Ellis, and Mother Lessie Randle, as well as the families of the deceased, have been asking these questions for a century.

For the African American community in Tulsa, the name "Reconciliation Way" symbolizes the unfinished work to achieve true healing and justice. It highlights the ongoing struggle for recognition, repair, and equality, and it underscores the importance of confronting the painful legacy in an honest and meaningful way. To achieve genuine reconciliation, meaningful actions must be taken to address the systemic racism and discrimination that continue to affect the Black community in Tulsa and across the country. This is why in 2022, my grandmother along with other survivors and their family members filed a lawsuit against the city of Tulsa for failing to recognize the massacre as a "public nuisance." The case continues to be litigated but a judgment in their favor will help Tulsa move beyond promise-filled words such as "reconciliation" and force the city to recognize and remedy the harm the massacre has had on its Black residents.

In the past, other survivors of the massacre and their descendants have come forward to tell their stories and seek justice, only to be met with dismissal, silencing, and retaliation. The trauma inflicted by the events of that fateful day in 1921 has left deep scars, and my grandmother, Viola Ford Fletcher, has also carried the weight of fear, hesitating to tell her truth for many years. She has seen how the city has buried and rewritten the stories of so many others. In a conversation with my grandmother about standing in her truth. I told her, "Don't let them bury your story." Our conversation inspired the title of this book, and it is a testament to her courage that she has chosen to share her memories.

On May 19, 2021, my grandmother testified before the US Congressional Subcommittee on the Constitution, Civil Rights, and Civil Liberties chaired by Rep. Sheila Jackson Lee of Texas. She concluded her emotional testimony with a call for justice, the same call for justice that she had been making since her mother, Lucinda, said a prayer for her long ago in a cotton field. After her testimony, she was invited to meet Vice President Kamala Harris with Uncle Redd and the family in a private meeting.

Dr. Martin Luther King Jr. said, "The arc of the moral universe is long, but it bends toward justice." I believe preserving these memories and telling the truth of survivors like my grandmother is crucial to helping our society bend towards justice. Change may take time, but it does happen. By confronting the dark chapters of our history, we can learn from the mistakes of the past and move toward a more equitable and just future. This book serves as a testament to the power of memory, the importance of truth-telling, and the resilience of those who have endured injustices and are still living today. It is a reminder that the stories of the past shape our present and have a lasting impact.

My hope is that my grandmother's story will enlighten future generations and give them the determination to seek justice wherever it is due.

Now is the time to make things right.

# PART I

# Let Me Tell My Story

## 1

# I Am Viola

I am the oldest known survivor of the 1921 Tulsa Race Massacre, and justice for me and those who came before me is long overdue! I stand on their shoulders, continuing the fight to be made whole from the terrible, horrific crimes committed against us. I stand for all those whose names have been lost in time and those resting in marked and unmarked graves.

I remember my mother praying as we worked out in an open cotton field on a sunshiny day. She prayed that I would live to be old enough to see justice for myself and all those who were victims of the massacre. That terrible event upended our lives and permanently changed the trajectory of our family and many others. I have lived through the diphtheria epidemic of 1921-1925, the Great Depression of 1929, the Dust Bowl of the 1930s, World War II, the Korean War, the Vietnam War, and other wars. I've seen the bubonic plague, witnessed polio eradicated with a miracle vaccine, saw on television the horrors of the Ebola plague in Africa, the bird flu, swine flu, the second measles outbreak, whooping cough,

HIV/AIDS, and now in the twenty-first century, the emergence of the deadly Covid-19 virus that has the whole world wearing masks and getting vaccines.

I've also seen Dr. Martin Luther King and other great Black leaders such as Malcolm X, Adam Clayton Powell, Congressman John Lewis, representatives Maxine Waters and Sheila Jackson-Lee, and I loved the poetry of Maya Angelou. I've seen men walk on the moon, and I've witnessed the election of our first Black president, Barack Obama, and marveled at the beauty and grace of his wife First Lady Michelle Obama, and two lovely daughters. Now, I have had the pleasure of seeing the first Black and East Indian and female Vice President, Kamala Harris, along with Nancy Pelosi, the former Speaker of the House of Representatives and a dynamic political force.

My God is a powerful God, and I know the injustices that my people and I have suffered in this nation will one day be atoned for. The nation has come a long way from those days when I was drinking water from a "colored-only" fountain as a child. I recently saw a hint of justice for one of our Black men, George Floyd, who was killed "live" on television by a uniformed police officer and three uniformed accomplices. However, the terrors of that night in 1921 came back, as if it was yesterday when I saw on the news three White men chase and gun down Ahmaud Arbery, an unarmed Black man, in broad daylight. Progress can take a life-time, and in my case, it has been 100 years and counting!

On May 10, 2020, because of Covid-19 restrictions, my wonderful grandchildren and great-grandchildren gave me a drive-by birthday party. I have never been more surprised! I didn't even know there was such a thing. But when you put your mind to it, all kinds of creative things are possible, even in the middle of a global pandemic. At my amazing drive-by birthday party, there were too many cars for me to count, including two fire engines from the Bartlesville Fire Department and patrol cars from the police department. The town's first responders were celebrating me with sirens blaring. It was so wonderful.

My grandchildren and I were interviewed on TV news, and it was that news coverage that put us back on the path toward justice. Right after that, my grandchildren were contacted by the law office of Damario Solomon-Simmons. Damario became our family attorney, representing me and my quest for justice for my family and all the lost souls of that unforgettable tragedy that destroyed my wonderful community of Greenwood. I realized that my mother spoke it into existence long ago when she prayed that I would live long enough to find justice. I was determined that I would not take my story to the grave without a fight. The world should know what happened, and that such a tragedy should never be repeated.

But then, my grandson Ike bought me a brand-new color television for my birthday in 2020. Some months later, I was shocked to see a mob attack the Capitol building on January 6, 2021, while Congress was in session preparing to sanction the vote count for the newly elected President, Joe Biden. And with that horrific scene, all of what occurred back in 1921 in Greenwood came flooding back into my mind.

CATALOG #1981.032.013, COLLECTION: Tulsa Race
Massacre, OBJECT: Postcard, Picture - DATE: 6/1/1921

## MY DAY IN CONGRESS

As I looked around the large circular room, I couldn't help but feel a mix of nerves and pride. Our lawyer, Damario, had worked hard to get us a chance to testify before a congressional subcommittee in Washington, D.C. I had never been to D.C. before, and I never thought. I would be there to tell my story on national television before the U.S. Government. The room was filled with representatives, lawyers, and reporters from various news outlets, all waiting to hear me and the other two survivors of the Tulsa Race Massacre speak our truth about what happened 100 years ago to the day.

I was there to ask my country to acknowledge what happened in Tulsa in 1921. For me, that was the whole point of my traveling to Washington, DC, and Congress; to ask for acknowledgment and, yes, atonement for the terrible things that were done to me, my family, and my people back then.

I sat in front of a small wooden table before the committee up on their podium. Damario sat next to me, and My brother, Redd, sat at an identical table a few feet from us. Everyone fell quiet as proceedings began. I wore a set of bulky black headphones over my ears so I could hear better.

The committee members introduced themselves one by one, their titles and positions echoing through the room. They spoke with professionalism and courtesy, acknowledging the gravity of the moment. They explained that the purpose of the hearing was to shed light on the painful history of the Tulsa Race Massacre and to seek justice and reparations for the survivors and descendants of Greenwood. Their opening statements lasted for about 20 minutes, during which they reflected on the significance of this hearing and the importance of addressing the long-standing injustices of the past.

They said some nice words, like how this was a historic moment and how looking back gives us the space to learn and do better. There was a lot of thanking and admonition against violence, even recounts of what history says happened that day. I remember one of them saying, *"What happened in Tulsa in 1921 was as wrong as can be."* It was an acknowledgment. Not an apology, but an acknowledgment.

When they finished, they welcomed me as the first to testify. All the cameras were on me, and I was nervous. But I was also proud. I knew I was representing not just myself but also the survivors and descendants of Greenwood. I wanted to honor their memory and ensure our stories were heard. I took a deep breath and began, *"I am Viola Ford Fletcher..."*

## 2

# The Massacre

On the eve of May 31, 1921, I returned home exhausted after a day of playing with neighbors and friends. My siblings and I had all just gone to bed. I don't know what time it was, but I remember I was half asleep when the catastrophe began.

I woke up thinking, "Who is making all that racket?" In my sleepy child brain, I thought someone was outside beating a rug. But who would be doing something like that so late at night?

BAM! BAM! BAM!

Mother hollered, using my nickname, "Vi! Get up, child, and stop asking questions! They are out there killing all the Black folk! Collect whatever you are able and let's get out of here! If we don't leave right now, we could end up dead."

Dead? What?

I was scared to death and didn't have any idea what was really going on. I just did as I was told, grabbing anything I could that seemed important to a seven-year-old. I would have grabbed more if I knew we would lose everything that night. Then we went outside and I saw the horrors and panicked faces with my own eyes. Everyone was screaming and running for their lives.

An airplane flew above us dropping firebombs. Men tossed torches from the street into the windows of people's homes. The buildings were burning from both top and bottom, all at once. Ash was falling on the streets like snow. It was very hard to breathe, and we were spitting up black soot from all the smoke.

Our brave and dedicated Black men ran like Paul Revere, knocking on people's doors, yelling for us to get out of our houses. The KKK, those white-hooded boogeymen – who in the light of day were court clerks, store owners, farmers, deputy sheriffs, city councilmen, farmers, city representatives, and businessmen – were coming for us. All those people jealous of our community's wealth had been "deputized" and provided with weapons by city officials, and they were coming to do us all harm

People often ask me, today, how we managed to escape the tragic events that occurred in Tulsa. There were six children in our family at the time – three girls and three boys (Jeurl, John, Cleon, Sarah, Hughes (Uncle Redd), and me. So we had a horse and buggy. Daddy loaded us all in the back as fast as he could and we fled.

My eyes burned and watered from the smoke and ash, but I could still see everything so clearly. People ran clinging to their loved ones toward the railroad or any path out of the town that was not overrun with armed White men. Some of them made it. So many did not. We passed piles of dead bodies heaped in the streets. Some of them had their eyes open, as though they were still alive, but they weren't.

I saw a white man screaming his allegiance to the KKK. One of his legs was shorter than the other and he walked with a noticeable limp. He held up his shotgun, pointed it, and blew a poor Black man's head clean off, right in front of us. It was a horrible thing for a child to see. The man's head exploded like a watermelon dropped off the rooftop of a barn.

That man with the limp turned in our direction and hollered at us, "Hey, you niggers!" he said. "Get out of this town, niggers! Greenwood belongs to us now." Then for good measure, he fired off a shotgun blast toward our buggy.

CATALOG #2012.065.007, COLLECTION: Tulsa
Race Massacre, OBJECT: Print, Photographic -
DATE: 6/1/1921

I don't know how Daddy managed to get us all out of there

with just a horse and buggy. Tulsa was engulfed in flames and ravaged by violence that night. The sounds of gunshots ringing and the screams of terrified people seemed to come from every direction. We had to navigate through the crowded and chaotic streets, avoiding all of the destruction.

Blood flowed everywhere in Greenwood like a stream full of wicked intentions. "Don't look!" My mother screamed. But we did anyway. White men and some women were looting houses or just burning them to the ground. I could hear that airplane somewhere overhead, but the smoke was so thick I couldn't make out its exact location.

I had no sense of direction and had to remember to breathe. We rode hard and fast, as Daddy cracked the whip. The horse and buggy were our only means of transportation, and Daddy urged the horse to go as fast as it could, pushing through the debris-strewn streets and avoiding the danger zones. My siblings and I were being violently thrown from side to side as we made our way out of Greenwood. Our tears appeared black as they rolled down our soot-covered cheeks.

Explosion after explosion boomed and more firebombs went off behind us. I believed that we were going to die. My little brother, Redd, screamed and cried. Jeurl was in total shock. Cleon wanted to get the gun and shoot back, and John and I were so scared we wet ourselves. Where were we going? How would we make it? My seven-year-old mental compass was just completely off.

It was a harrowing journey, with our hearts pounding in our chests We were desperate to leave the chaos behind and find safety elsewhere. The only thing I can say for certain is how grateful we all were that God had seen us out. And so we rode through the night for who knows how long.

We eventually landed in a wooded area outside of Claremore, Oklahoma (which we didn't know at the time was the state headquarters of the Ku Klux Klan) and took shelter in a tent.

\* \* \*

The questions I had then remain to this day. How could you just give a mob of violent, crazed, racist people a bunch of deadly weapons and allow them—no, encourage them—to go out and kill innocent Black folks and demolish a whole community? How much evil and pure jealousy-driven hatred do you need to have in your heart, to do the things they did?

CATALOG #1982.033.003, COLLECTION: Tulsa Race
Massacre, OBJECT: Print, Photographic - DATE: 6/1/1921

As it turns out, we were victims of a lie. As the story goes, a young Black man named Dick Rowland, who was an employee of a department store in downtown Tulsa had been falsely accused of accosting a White woman. He had been arrested but then released because the woman in question denied that he had hurt her in any way and refused to press charges. This situation was used as a scapegoat by some of Tulsa's White residents who were envious of Greenwood's prosperity. They were hell-bent on taking everything we had, including our livelihood, and our lives.

CATALOG #1977.025.004, COLLECTION: Tulsa Race Massacre, OBJECT: Print, Photographic - DATE: 6/1/1921

## 3

## Before the Storm

I was born in Comanche County, Oklahoma. Our family proudly considered ourselves "double natives" or true natives, often visiting Big Hill, an elevated place that the old natives once used as a lookout point. We also enjoyed exploring the townships near Fairfax in Osage County, close to Pawhuska.

Our grandmother, maternal grandmother Dora Love, had migrated to Oklahoma from Austin, Texas. Granny Love was a remarkable woman, descended from Native Americans (Cherokee, Blackfoot, and Creek) and African Americans. She was what people at that time called a "mulatto," a term derived from Spanish and Portuguese meaning "mule." It became a derogatory slur against those born of a mixed-race union. Despite facing discrimination, Granny Love always chose to live near the Native American reservation as she wanted to stay close to her people. Granny Love lived a remarkable 100 years, from 1871 to 1971 when she peacefully passed away and earned her wings in heaven.

My mother Lucinda Ellis

My mother, Lucinda Ellis, was a beautiful woman who married my hardworking father. Together they had a family. However, they later divorced, and she remarried my stepfather, Henry Ellis. He was a skilled man, adept at various trades. With his dedication, hard work, and determination, we finally settled into a nice home in the Greenwood area of Tulsa where we had everything we needed. This is where I spent most of my young life, until the night of the massacre.

\* \* \*

The past is still as vivid to me as the present.

I remember being a young girl in Greenwood and how it was a lively and vibrant community where we had everything we needed – churches, lawyers, doctors, nurses, pharmacists, soda shops, teachers, beauty parlors, grocers, department stores, places to eat, banks, etc. We had it all. We thrived despite the challenges of Jim Crow segregation.

John Wesley Williams and wife, Loula Cotten Williams, and their son, William Danforth Williams

One of my fondest memories was after a day of fishing, using a limb off of an elm tree as our fishing rod. We would bait it with salt pork and worms we dug up, and then have a good old fish fry. We had so much fun, laughing and enjoying the simple pleasures of life. This was back when movies were silent, and listening to the radio meant using our imagination to paint pictures in our minds.

I remember playing with my wooden dolls and a rubber ball and jacks with my friends, and how our fathers and uncles would make delicious homemade ice cream. The women in the community would bake pies, pastries, and layer cakes, filling the air with their sweet aroma. We would have sleepovers at each other's homes, feeling safe and loved in our close-knit community. We danced in the sun and even in the rain, finding joy in every moment.

We went to church every Wednesday night and every Sunday without exception, finding strength in our shared faith. We were truly blessed beyond measure. Our churches were at the heart of our community. They provided a place for fellowship, socializing, and recreation. We would have picnics, socials, and other events, and the church choirs and cultural activities were always a source of inspiration and enjoyment.

In those days, we lived simply but well. Families would barter goods – one family may have had milk to offer and another fruit or eggs – creating a system of exchange that sustained us. Some families even made liquor or "spirits" as we called it. Banks and prosperous businessmen would help with loans or services to start businesses. We didn't need to look beyond Greenwood for most services, and they were reasonably priced. Every job, no matter how big or small, was performed with pride and importance. We were tight-knit; everyone looked out for each other and we shared everything we had.

Music was a big part of our lives. We had our own jazz bands and blues singers, and live performances were a regular occurrence. Folks would gather at local venues or social clubs, dancing and enjoying the rhythm of the music, and it brought us so much joy and a sense of togetherness.

Sports were also a big hit in Greenwood. We had our own baseball teams and organized sports events, and both kids and adults would participate. It was not just about the competition, but also about the camaraderie and having fun. We would cheer for our teams, and the community would come together to support our athletes.

We eagerly anticipated community celebrations and events. Juneteenth was a special occasion in our community, with parades, picnics, and other festivities designed to bring people together and honor our heritage.

It was common to visit friends and neighbors, share meals and conversations or take walks in the neighborhood. We valued the time we spent together, the shared stories, and the laughter.

I am the fourth from the left. My sister Jeurl is behind me, and my brother John has on the coveralls

Greenwood allowed us all to dream, to envision the promise of America. And within a few hours, the dream became a nightmare. In hindsight, I can now understand why those who attacked our community used firebombs and torches. It would not be enough to beat us physically. We would have bounced back from that. But Greenwood represented Black progress and autonomy. Tulsa's White community at the time held our success in contempt, viewing it as a threat to their own. To burn our community to the ground was the only way to truly destroy it . . . and everything we stood for.

The residents of Greenwood were a people rich in heritage, love, and provision. It was a community defined by its unique cultural fabric and strong spirit. The memories of Greenwood and its close-knit community are etched in my heart, my blood even. But now, in the hundred years since, I see those happy days as the calm before the storm.

4

# A Step Toward Justice

"When my family was forced to leave Tulsa, I lost my chance at an education. I never finished school past the fourth grade." I said, reading from the speech my team helped me prepare.

The congressional hearing room was silent. No one interrupted as I shared my story. I could feel the emotions welling up inside me. It was a mix of anger, frustration, and sadness. Even though it was long past my time to be angry, I needed to say what had been inside for nearly a century. I lived most of my life in poverty, and racial discrimination and violence were responsible. White Tulsans with a chip on their shoulder, whom the local government protected, took my home and countless opportunities to better my life.

With my lawyer Damario Solomon-Simmons turning pages for me, I continued, "I have never made much money. My country, state, and city took a lot from me. Despite this, I spent time supporting the war effort in the shipyards of California. Most of my life, I was a domestic worker serving White families. . . ."

Just as most White Americans may never truly understand the plight of refugees, they may also never fully comprehend the challenges of living in poverty and facing discrimination as a Black woman. It's a reality that has shaped my life in profound ways, from struggling to make ends meet to being treated as a second-class citizen in my own country. I grew up in a country that often treated me as cheap or free manual labor, relegated to low-paying jobs and facing constant discrimination. It was a thankless existence, and I often felt overlooked, disregarded, and marginalized. The inequality and injustice I witnessed and experienced left a mark on me. I knew that my life could have been different if not for the systemic racism and discrimination that permeated every aspect of society.

Yet, I remained resilient, determined, and hopeful. I refused to let the circumstances define me or limit my potential. I found strength in my heritage, culture, and community, and I drew inspiration from the tireless efforts of other civil rights activists who had fought for change. I kept my faith in the Most High, and I believed—and still do believe—that he has sustained me all these 108 years so that I might see justice.

When people think of justice, they think of scales, the image on all our court buildings. They think of balance or things being set right. They think of criminals going to jail. It is a simple concept, "If you do the crime, you do the time."

Unfortunately, this is not how justice is issued for everyone in this country. In 1921, when a mob murdered our fathers and brothers and sisters and mothers for two days, they said it was to punish one Black man for allegedly assaulting a White woman in an elevator. They said it was to punish one Black man for allegedly assaulting a White woman in an elevator. They were seeking justice. But what kind of justice destroys an entire community and kills innocent people? That is not justice. That is war and terrorism. And because of that, the scales are grossly imbalanced.

People were irrevocably harmed, and the perpetrators answered to nobody but themselves. They walked away believing they did a fine job scaring us uppity Black folks out of "their" town to maintain the "order" of white supremacy. But what of us who had our lives and dreams destroyed? What about those of us who lost every reasonable opportunity to make it in this country or to see our descendants thriving in our lifetime? Where do we look to balance the scales?

Many Americans voted for President Trump in 2016 because of his slogan: Make America Great Again. I laughed. In a way, his supporters were looking for some kind of justice, to balance the scales and reclaim some things they think they have lost. But what many of these people were chanting for, especially the older generations, was a return to a world in which White people could act with impunity. Despite a lifetime of service and patriotism, my brother Redd and I have yet to see the most basic benefits of American citizenship. We should have been saying "Let's make America great . . . for all of us."

My mother used to say, "What's done in the dark will eventually come to light." Keeping dark secrets will prevent someone from entering heaven. The public nuisance case must be abated. The city of Tulsa must take responsibility for its past actions and make amends through reparations and reconciliation. When we come together, we become stronger as a community.

At a recent court hearing, it came to light that the city possesses land where prominent Black-owned businesses once stood. I am convinced that these sites should be dedicated to establishing new Black businesses, paving the way for the next generation of Black Wall Street. Undeniably, creating jobs within the community is of great value.

Additionally, I propose considering the possibility of directing a portion of the profits generated by these new businesses to a victim compensation fund. In my family, we trust in common sense and hold fast to the belief that where there's a will, there's a way. In my opinion, a united Tulsa that offers opportunities for all will undoubtedly result in a brighter future for everyone.

Justice for me is whatever it takes to balance the scales. We—those of us who have survived these 100 long years—are the living victims of the largest hate crime in US history and we have not even received a true acknowledgment of what happened. While the mayor has apologized, he has never apologized to our faces.

To echo what I said before Congress, I have lived through the massacre every day since. Our country may forget this event. They may treat it as history. But I cannot. It is a part of my life's story, the same as if you or your neighbor were robbed or beaten yesterday. I will not forget when I close my eyes. And other survivors do not. And our descendants do not.

As I and my brother and Mother Randle sat before the congressional subcommittee to tell our story, we were also prepared to ask for what was taken. Our livelihoods and our opportunities. Not only did I not get to finish my education, but many of our descendants did not get to go to college. My brothers and my grandson both served in the military to try and create new opportunities and remove the blight left on our bloodline.

We were seeking the chance to make it right. At that time, the chance was all we could fight for because the courts had refused to hear every case brought forth on the massacre. There was never even a trial to present a case for the Black families in Tulsa who have been so discarded and disenfranchised. Not even during the civil rights movement did our families get the opportunity to be heard.

I sat before the congressional subcommittee reminded of how easy it was for those in power to deny the truth, to dismiss the violence and destruction that took place during the Tulsa massacre. "For 70 years, the city of Tulsa and its chamber of commerce denied that it happened," I said, as I approached the end of my testimony, "as if we, the survivors, didn't witness it with our own eyes." But there we were, Mother Randle, my brother Hughes Van Ellis, and I, living testimonies of this history that could not be ignored. It lived with us.

Attempts have been made to uplift Greenwood, but time and again, funding has been diverted, legislation denied, and benefits not paid out. All we could ask for was for the government, which we have all served in some capacity, to open its doors and allow us to be heard.

In front of Congress, Mother Randle, Uncle Redd, and I demanded recognition for our history—not just for Black Americans, but for White Americans and all Americans. We wanted those responsible to be held accountable for the atrocities committed against us and an assurance that this part of our history does not repeat itself. I hoped that this Congress would listen to our stories, learn, and take action. I wanted a commitment to ensuring a just and equitable society for everyone. That, to me, would be some justice.

It was time for justice to be served, and for our truth and pain to be recognized. This was not just about compensation (that was important too), but about the abatement of the public nuisance created by the massacre and the systemic racism that had persisted across the years that followed. Justice for us meant more than just words or empty promises. It meant acknowledging the deep-rooted inequalities and injustices that had plagued Black communities for centuries. It meant recognizing the contributions and resilience of Black Americans and addressing the systemic racism that continued to perpetuate inequality in all aspects of our lives.

After I finished speaking, there was a brief pause. Damario asked if there was anything else I wanted to share. I said no, and the committee members thanked me for sharing my story. The room swelled in applause and we received a standing ovation. I felt a sense of relief. It was a small victory, but an important one. I had spoken my truth, and I knew that my words had made an impact.

I would never forget testifying before a congressional subcommittee. I was grateful for the opportunity to share my story with the world. Our fight for justice was far from over, but I felt better about pushing forward until our voices were fully heard and justice finally served.

The only question left was, "Would Congress do anything?"

# PART II

# A Life Lived

5

# Life in Aftermath

The horses were exhausted when we finally stopped. Daddy damn near beat the animals half to death. But by the grace of God, we escaped bloodline extinction. We ended up in Claremore, Oklahoma with no more than the clothes on our backs, and I still had on soiled underwear.

We had left behind our cherished belongings, our home, and our community. The weight of the tragedy was heavy, and the scars of the horrific events were still fresh, both physically and emotionally. As we sought refuge in Claremore, a town we had never been to before, the uncertainty of our situation was overwhelming. We had no place to call home, no familiar faces to rely on, and no idea of what the future held for us. We were strangers in a strange land, trying to make sense of a new reality that had been forced upon us.

A sense of loss and confusion rushed over me as I thought about what had happened to my home. A vibrant and bustling community was now a smoldering ruin. Streets that were once filled with familiar faces and sounds of laughter were now empty and silent, except for the distant echoes of sirens and cries of anguish. I couldn't comprehend why such violence and hatred had been unleashed upon innocent people. It was clearly the devil's work.

For years, we lived out of a tent, and it was not easy. We eventually settled into our new home in rural Oklahoma, adapting to a more natural way of living. Our tent was basic, devoid of modern conveniences like electricity or running water. Whereas today we are used to modern plumbing, back then, farms and farmland used outhouses. And if you didn't have an outhouse or if it was full, you could wander off and do your business wherever. The women needed to be more cautious so three of us would go out at the same time. If one needed more privacy, the other two held up a large quilt for cover.

The quilts we used were not fancy. They were patchwork quilts that were often passed down from generation to generation and were made from a variety of materials, including scraps of fabric and old clothing that had been repurposed. The result was a beautiful tapestry of colors and patterns that was as functional as it was visually striking. Elders would cut and stitch the scraps together to create intricate patterns and designs, creating something out of what others might see as nothing.

What I didn't realize then was that this tradition of patchwork quilting was deeply rooted in African American and Native American culture. Quilting was a way for our ancestors to use every part of the fabric and repurpose it into something useful. It was a way to create warmth and privacy but also a way to express creativity and artistry. To this day, I remain in awe of the ingenuity and resilience of the people I grew up with.

Quilts weren't the only things that we repurposed. We made use of everything we had, from wagon wheels to old pieces of wood. It was a matter of survival. We were poor and constantly on the move. We had to be resourceful and nothing was wasted. This same spirit of resourcefulness is what led to so many Black inventors throughout history. When faced with limited resources and little support, Black inventors had to get creative and find solutions to problems on their own. They saw potential where others did not and were able to turn even the most unlikely materials into something useful. My father was like that, and I will always be grateful for how he taught us to be creative.

We always tried to make the best of our situation. The Oklahoma weather posed additional difficulties. On hot days, we sought shelter from the blazing sun, finding shade under trees or improvised coverings. At night, we huddled together for warmth, using thick blankets and layers of clothing to protect us from the cold.

These experiences also brought emotional challenges. As Black individuals in predominantly White communities, we were met with stares and suspicion and often treated like gypsies. It was a difficult chapter in our lives, but it also served as a testament to our resilience and determination.

My mother, Dora Love, mother was Native American. Granny Dora, her mother, showed us how to use medicinal herbs and spices for gamey food. I thank God for their heritage and wisdom because we needed it to live off of the land and survive in the wilderness. We set traps made from string, sticks, and rocks to catch rabbits and other animals. We picked blueberries, blackberries, and mulberries, and made broom wheat tea to prevent us from getting sick with colds and coughs. We would boil the broom wheat and then add honey and corn whiskey, and with that home remedy, you would feel better for sure. Wild onions scrambled together with eggs was our favorite breakfast meal. At night, believe it or not, you could catch enough lightning bugs to put in a mason jar, to make you a glow light.

As we settled into our new life as sharecroppers, I found comfort in the teachings of Granny Dora and the skills she had passed down to us. Her wisdom and guidance helped me find a sense of belonging and purpose. It taught me how important family and community are, the value of resourcefulness, and the beauty of nature. I learned to appreciate the simple joys of life once again. Though the scars of what happened in Tulsa, and the pain of losing loved ones still lingered, I found strength in the resilience of my family. We still had each other.

My father quickly found work for us as sharecroppers. We would work hard from sunup to sundown, all for just a dollar a day. We traveled from town to town, handling livestock and doing fieldwork that included picking cotton which is a grueling task. It requires long hours of labor under the scorching sun, with fingers constantly pricked by sharp cotton bolls. The physical strain is immense, and the toll it takes on the body is evident in sore muscles, calloused hands, and weary souls. As Black individuals in the Jim Crow era, we had to endure physical challenges like picking cotton, but the discrimination, mistreatment, and low wages we faced were degrading and added to our burden.

One day while working in the fields, I fell to my knees and started crying. My mother was alarmed, of course, and asked me, "What's wrong, child?"

CATALOG #1984.002.024, COLLECTION: Tulsa Race
Massacre, OBJECT: Print, Photographic - DATE: 6/1/1921

With tears streaming down my young face, I told her, "I miss my friends, and our church, and the movie theater, and our ice cream parlor." I missed it all. The railroads and the funeral parlor too. I understood why we had to leave everything behind. Still, I felt a deep longing for the familiarity and comfort of our home, our community, and the simple joys of life we had before the massacre. This was life as a refugee.

Several months passed, and we welcomed two new additions to our family, my twin siblings Albert and Mary. They were born healthy with the help of midwives, who possess ancestral knowledge passed down from other midwives. Thank God for them because they were an essential support system that helped bring Black babies into the world as safely as possible under all kinds of unfortunate and challenging circumstances.

Lucinda holding twins Mary and Albert

During that period, our family experienced a severe outbreak of whooping cough. The challenging living conditions, limited access to medical care, and constant exposure to the harsh weather facilitated the rapid spread of the disease. Every member of our family contracted it, including little Mary. Our beloved Granny Dora, who had inherited a traditional and safe recipe from generations of midwives, prepared the tonic to aid us in this terrible illness.

Remarkably, Granny Dora's tonic contained an essential ingredient: cannabis oil. Cannabis held a significant role in the traditional medicinal practices of numerous Native American tribes, including Granny Dora's. Its historical usage for medicinal purposes was extensive, with different parts of the plant used for various ailments. Leaves and flowers, for instance, were commonly used to create teas, tinctures, and poultices to alleviate pain, fever, and inflammation.

In our case, cannabis oil was incorporated into the tonic to alleviate the symptoms of respiratory illnesses, including asthma, bronchitis, and the whooping cough that afflicted us. It effectively reduced and, at times, eliminated the coughing fits, allowing our bodies the opportunity to heal naturally.

Every afflicted family member received the tonic and experienced a full recovery, except for baby Mary. Despite our earnest efforts, we were unable to save her. Although the trusted recipe was generally considered harmless, it possessed sedative properties. Concerns arose when administering it to a young, already lethargic child. Could her delicate body handle it? What if she didn't wake up? Tragically, Mary passed away at the tender age of two or three. I cannot help but contemplate whether administering the medicine could have saved her. This ancestral remedy was our solace, easing our symptoms and rescuing the rest of us.

Losing my baby sister Mary to a preventable disease was an excruciating experience. It served as an ever present reminder of the harsh realities and inequalities that Native Americans and Black people endured during those times. Even now, the thought of it fills me with anger.

My family worked tirelessly to make ends meet. The grueling work, long hours, and constant moving took a toll on us. I thought often of all the black businesses back home in Greenwood. I missed all the hard-working people and the positive examples of free black enterprise that they represented.

After a few years, I complained to my mother that I would never find a husband if my hands continued getting scratched and cut up doing this rough sharecropper work. Tears welled up in my eyes as I recalled my mother's response. "Dear Lord, please allow my daughter to live long enough to receive justice!" My mother prayed earnestly out loud, and I whispered "Amen" silently, echoing her prayers.

I am grateful that that prayer remained important to us. We never lost our faith in God or our ability to worship him on Sundays. And we always found a way to gather on Sundays.

Even though we were nomadic, we were often in communities with other sharecroppers on the same land for as little as a week to as long as a few months at a time. Families would bring together blankets and poles to pitch big tents like they did in Biblical days. Then we used whatever we could—overturned wagons, buckets, tires, you name it—as stools and benches to sit on. There was always somebody who considered himself a preacher, even if they never went to school for it. So that is how we would have service. It was not extravagant. No one dressed up like we would in a real church, but that was not the point. It was about renewing our spirit. Besides, I am a firm believer that God is in you, in each of us. The Word says, "Where two or three are gathered in my name, there shall I be in the midst of them—even so I am in the midst of you."

Sundays were also days that we had the best meals, based on what we were able to save or scavenge throughout the week. Sometimes we could sacrifice a chicken or a rabbit. Sometimes we traded and bartered with people from other groups. Most often, there was a sharing of resources. Everyone chipped in to bring the different parts of the meal so. It was the only way we could all eat. It's how we survived.

As sharecroppers, we were never in the same place with the same people for very long, and it was difficult to form lifelong friendships this way. However, we still formed alliances. Most of the time that was the only way to get everything you needed. Landowners did not offer a high enough wage to support the family. You had to talk with the other groups to get ingredients, spices, medicine, and information.

You could find out from other families if an employer was fair or even safe before agreeing to any work arrangements. Some employers used debt and false accusations to keep workers bound to the land for little or no pay. Some would take the women—and even men—to the houses and rape them as a way to settle these alleged debts. Fortunately, my family was able to avoid employers like this because we made good allies, and my father was smart about our arrangements. Still, I know we all dreamed of days when this lifestyle would end.

One morning, I found myself lying in a wheat field looking at the clouds, One of them looked just like an elephant from Africa. I wondered what it must be like to live in a place like that, live in Africa, and live in harmony with nature and animal life. It was probably just like the way Native peoples here lived, as Granny Dora always told us. I remember praying that one day I would go and see Africa for myself. It became a lifelong dream of mine.

Weeks later, on one of our sojourns searching for work from farm to farm, I saw one of my old elementary school friends from Greenwood. It was one of the happiest moments I'd experienced since our escape from the catastrophe. Her name was Deborah, and when we saw each other, we hugged so tight we could've broken each other's ribs.

Young Viola - 1939

We both wanted to know if either had seen any of the other boys and girls from our school, but we were the first and only ones both of us had seen in eight long years. I noticed that her hands were as scratched up and wounded as mine. Nevertheless, I was so happy to see Deborah those years later. That was one of the few happy moments I had out there in the wilderness. Deborah was a true friend and years later, I named my only daughter after her.

Amidst the hardships, I held on to the memories of our past and the hope for a better future. I remembered the prayers of my mother and the teachings of my grandmother, and I remained determined to seek justice and create a better life for myself and my daughter, carrying the strength and resilience of my community with me wherever I went.

* * *

In 1929, the world was experiencing what the newspapers were calling "The Great Depression". As far as I was concerned, we colored folks were in a state of depression well before the economic collapse on Wall Street. Their financial and investment losses had people jumping out of windows and committing suicide. They were committing suicide over money. It was clear that the economic collapse had hit them hard, and the affluence that some enjoyed had become a thing of the past.

The economic collapse only compounded our existing challenges with limited job opportunities, reduced wages, and discrimination. Despite these obstacles, our community showed resilience, relying on our ingenuity and community networks to make ends meet. We were happy to just have gravy and bread, which was a simple daily meal for us.

On birthdays and holidays, we would kill and eat a chicken. I still remember the excitement and anticipation of those special occasions, when my family would carefully choose a chicken from our modest backyard flock and prepare it with love. The scent of roasted chicken would fill the air, and we would gather around the table, grateful for the bounty before us. It was a rare and cherished treat that brought us together as a family during those difficult times.

If Momma ran out of flour for biscuits, she made hot water cornbread, and sometimes the gravy was made from cornmeal instead of flour. I can still taste the warm, crispy edges of the cornbread and the rich, savory flavor of the cornmeal gravy that Momma would pour over it. It was a simple yet delicious meal that sustained us, even when resources were scarce.

Instead of bacon, we ate salt pork and beans. Salt pork, a cheaper cut of meat with a high-fat content, was a staple in our meals. Momma would slow-cook it with beans and season it with herbs and spices, creating a flavorful and filling dish that kept our bellies full. We used every part of the animals we slaughtered. Neighbors who had cows would share their milk and butter, and we would trade or barter for other food items we didn't have.

The adults ate first during meals and whatever was left was fed to the kids. It was a hard lesson in prioritizing who ate first. But it also taught us the value of sharing and looking out for one another.

No part of any hog or animal was wasted, and thank God rabbits like to reproduce. We ate chicken feet, turkey necks, pig's feet, nose, ears, chitterlings, "from the rooter to the tooter" as we liked to say. They may have been less popular cuts of meat, but we found creative ways to prepare them so that we could enjoy them.

We also used cane poles and tree limbs for fishing, which was both a pastime and a means of sustenance for our family. I would spend hours by the river or the lake, casting my homemade pole and patiently waiting for a bite. When someone caught a fish it was a moment of triumph and pride. It was a reminder that nature could provide for us, even in difficult times.

We grew our own fruits and vegetables. We saved the seeds from all our crops, so we didn't have to buy any for the next season. We carefully tended to our backyard garden, nurturing the plants with care and patience. The joy of seeing the first sprouts break through the soil and the satisfaction of harvesting fresh produce for our meals were priceless. It was a labor of love and a way to ensure that we had nutritious food on our plates, even when times were tough.

At the age of 16, I went back to that horrible place of my nightmares: Tulsa, Oklahoma. I was going to live with my now-married older sister Jeurl. Jeurl married George Ishem in Wichita, Kansas. George found work back in Tulsa and had relatives there.

My brother-in-law George Ishem

The trauma of the massacre still haunted me long after we had escaped Tulsa. The horrors of that night were etched into my mind, replaying like an unending movie ree. They disrupted my sleep and invaded my waking thoughts. I would often wake up drenched in sweat, my heart pounding in my chest as a scene of flames, gunshots, and screams played out in my mind. I could never forget the charred remains of our once-thriving community, the smoke billowing in the air, and the terror-stricken faces of my neighbors.

The trauma wasn't limited to my own experiences. My older

relatives would often wake up in the middle of the night, screaming about people burning down their houses and attacking their loved ones. Their fear was present, and their anguish was etched on their faces. The psychological wounds of that fateful night ran deep, and they continued to reverberate through our lives long after the ashes had settled.

As I decided to return to Tulsa, I was plagued with questions and uncertainties. What would I find there? Would the scars of the massacre still be visible? How would I navigate the lingering racism? The fear of the unknown gnawed at me, but I also didn't want to let anyone stop me from doing what I wanted or needed to. My sister Jeurl did not want to return to Tulsa, nor did I. George, who could put a 12-gauge shotgun together blindfolded, came from a large family and assured us he could protect us.

Upon my return to Tulsa, I was greeted by a city that had changed, yet was still very much the same. The Greenwood District had been reduced to ashes, with only a few remnants of the once vibrant community remaining. The streets that bustled with life just a few years ago now carried the weight of trauma. The destruction that was left Greenwood was just the visible version of the scars that were inside of us.

Sometimes I couldn't escape the flashbacks and memories that flooded my mind as I walked the streets of Tulsa. The familiar sights and sounds brought back a flood of emotions, and I found myself transported back to that dark night when everything changed. The smell of smoke and the sound of gunshots echoed in my ears, and I could feel my heart race as I relived the trauma once again. It was as if the wounds that had been buried deep within me had been ripped open, and I would be left grappling with the pain and grief all over again.

Despite this, I still wanted to have my life. I went to work for a department store named Kress. I was one fine-looking young Black lady, with scratches still on her hands from working in those fields. With my head held high and without any formal education, I worked as a decorator, creating window displays and cleaning the entire store. I felt proud to be working.

Daily reminders that I was not fully respected or accepted were all around me at work. The cafeteria was segregated, with White employees enjoying their lunch breaks in a clean area above ground, while colored employees like me were relegated to a smelly basement. The bathrooms were also segregated, but I had to clean them all as part of my job.

One day, while stocking shelves, I heard a voice that made my blood run cold. It was a distinguished voice. I looked up to find a White male studying my physique. The voice sounded all too familiar, and as I looked down, I noticed that he had different soles on his feet, with one leg noticeably longer than the other. It hit me like a ton of bricks—this was one of the people I remembered from that horrific night of our escape from Greenwood. He had been part of the racist White mob that had brutally killed a Black man with a shotgun.

Overwhelmed by fear, anger, and trauma, I trembled violently. I quickly moved to a different aisle, trying to compose myself, but the memories came flooding back with full force.

I couldn't contain my emotions, and I ended up wetting myself. It was embarrassing, but I knew I had to clean up the mess. After all, it was my job to clean the whole store, no matter how difficult it was at that moment.

As I looked at the man who had been part of the mob that had terrorized our community, a surge of anger and frustration welled up within me. How was it fair that he and others like him could go about their lives without consequence as if they had never committed such atrocities? How could these monsters be so smug? How could they go unpunished? It wasn't fair, but I trusted that someday, God Almighty would settle the debt.

Until then, I wasn't going to let racism stop me from living and being God's child. I knew who I served, and he is a redeemer of lost things and stolen land. It was out of my control, but not His.

I was at Kress for two years before I met Robert Fletcher, a kind and charming man. He worked in a nearby bakery, and he would often come to the store with delicious pies and pastries as a way to win my heart. He invited me on dates, and we would go to the movies or take walks by the river. I enjoyed his company, and we grew closer with each passing day.

Despite our budding relationship, I was hesitant about the idea of marriage. I had seen firsthand the challenges and injustices faced by Black people in our community, and I was cautious about committing to a lifelong union. However, Robert was persistent and patient, and he won over my family with his sincerity and kindness.

One day, I went to visit my mother in the countryside, seeking her advice. She shared her belief that having another man in the family would bring stability and support. Her words resonated with me, and I started to see Robert in a new light. We continued to live together, with my mother assuming we were already married. But deep down, I struggled with my own reservations, torn between my love for Robert and my concerns about the world we lived in.

After much contemplation and soul-searching, I finally

consented to marry Robert Fletcher. It was a leap of faith, but I hoped that our love could overcome the obstacles and injustices that surrounded us. I took comfort in the fact that we were in this together. I was willing to face whatever challenges came our way, hand-in-hand with Robert, as we entered this new chapter of our lives.

Viola Ford Fletcher

## 6

## Married Life

The wedding took place in Tulsa during World War II. It was a humble affair at a time when the dust bowl and the impacts of the Great Depression were felt deeply. Robert and I had little money for anything big, but we were content to exchange our vows and start our life together. We went down to the courthouse and signed the papers, and I became Mrs. Viola Ford Fletcher.

My new husband's brother had moved to California with his wife, and they encouraged us to move there as well, promising better treatment for colored folks and higher pay. It was a big move. I would have to leave the life I knew, my family, and the few friends I had made. But it wasn't much of a choice. Back then, you had to follow the money and take work where you could.

Life in Tulsa was as bad as it had ever been for us. Truthfully, I was also tired of living so close to the ruins of my childhood home. Being so close to that and the perpetrators, those above the law walking around as if they had done no wrong, weighed on my soul. Murderers and thieves lived unpunished, while we the survivors, were left to bear the scars and endure the indignities of being treated as inferior citizens.

Robert and I weighed the risks and benefits and eventually decided to take a leap of faith toward a fresh start. We traveled west by bus and train. In California, racial discrimination was present, but it was not as obvious or harsh as in Tulsa. Robert and I were able to find work right away. I took a job, of all places, at the Kress department store. This Kress was different from the one in Tulsa. For one thing, I was allowed to eat in the same cafeteria, even at the counter. This was a significant change for me, as I was treated more like a human being. And the pay was higher, which provided us with some financial stability.

My brother Albert

While I settled in California, my brothers Redd and Albert were both away fighting in the war. Redd served in the United States Army, assigned to an all-Black, segregated anti-aircraft battalion in far-off Burma, one of the most violent theaters of conflict in the entire history of World War II. Troops from four foreign powers, Britain, Japan, China, and the United States were involved in bloody battles that left deep physical and psychological scars on those fighting there, including my brother Redd. On the other hand, Albert was in the US Navy as a torpedo man, assigned to fight against enemy submarines.

At first, Black soldiers served in segregated units with limited opportunities for combat roles. The majority of Black soldiers were assigned to support roles, such as service units or labor battalions. But as the fighting went on, I remember how the White folks here complained that White soldiers were fighting and dying while Black soldiers held the "safe" roles. I think many of them were afraid all the White men would die and only Black men would come home, so many Black soldiers were assigned to munitions battalions due to the dangerous work involved.

Because I had two brothers in the war, I—like many Americans with a deep patriotic spirit and a desire to support our fighting men— went to work in Los Angeles at Cals Shipyard, hoping it would contribute to bringing my brothers home safely. I was considered smart enough to be trained as a welder and became one of the original "Rosy the Riveters" (like Rose Will Monroe, featured in Life magazine). Over 40,000 people worked at that shipyard. It was remarkable that 85% of those working on-site were women.

As a woman working during World War II, I faced many challenges and experiences that were unique to the time. The war created a need for a massive workforce to support the military. Women like me stepped up to fill the gaps left by men who had gone off to fight. We worked in jobs that were traditionally considered for men such as welding, riveting, and other heavy labor roles.

California Shipbuilding work badge

One of the challenges was breaking through gender stereotypes and facing discrimination. Many people had preconceived notions that women were not capable of handling physically demanding jobs. However, we proved them wrong by showing our strength, determination, and skills. We had to earn the respect of our male colleagues and supervisors, and it was not always easy. But we were motivated by a deep sense of patriotism and the desire to contribute to the war effort. We took pride in our roles. Our work was significant.

The work was tough, with long hours, physically demanding tasks, and exposure to hazardous materials. We had to adapt quickly to the demands of the job and learn new skills. Most of us women were also expected to maintain our houses and take care of our families. It was a juggling act, and many of us faced immense pressure and exhaustion.

Even with the challenges, working at the shipyard during the war was a rewarding experience. It finally allowed me to make a decent wage. I earned enough to send money home to my mother and my sister Jeurl in Tulsa to help with her children. I also rented a bedroom in someone's house, and later I moved to a garage apartment for more privacy. This was important to me because, in the rented bedroom, I noticed on more than one occasion that some of my undergarments had been moved.

The shipyard operated around the clock in multiple shifts. Many people just slept in their cars and worked overtime. As a welder, I had to wear a heavy leather suit and steel helmet hood, and the equipment was so cumbersome and thick that I would sweat from head to toe. Although wearing protective equipment was necessary, it was also uncomfortably hot. On the upside, it helped me to keep my figure, as I cleaned up well, according to the gentlemen.

At the shipyard, I was mostly treated as an equal and judged based on my abilities as a welder rather than the color of my skin. I was proud to be one of the many Black women who contributed to the war effort and helped to break down barriers. I worked alongside women from all walks of life. We formed strong bonds and developed a sense of belonging through our shared purpose of supporting our troops overseas. It was a huge step up from share-cropping cotton.

In 1945, the whistle blew, alerting us to the announcement. Finally, the war was over! All the work came to a complete stop. People dropped their shovels and tools right then and there. We started clapping, singing, dancing, and praising God, rejoicing because that bloody war was finally over. But it was a bittersweet moment. As I celebrated the end of the war, I also faced challenges in my personal life. The toll of the war, the long hours and physical demands of my job, and the strain of being away from my family had taken its toll. My marriage was on shaky ground.

My husband, Robert, was jealous because I was making more money than he was and because I opted to support my mother, sister, and blind Aunty in Tulsa. He began drinking more alcohol and became physically abusive. I think his problem stemmed from the fact that he was rejected for military service. I believe this diminished his manhood, and he took that out on me. All his other brothers were in the military, and he just felt less of a man. But I wasn't going to let him abuse me. My sister Jeurl wrote often, encouraging me to form an escape plan. She always said: "We survived the massacre, so we can survive anything!" The only problem was that she wrote to me on postcards and Robert had seen some of them and got angry about what she wrote. He beat me up when I refused to show him any of the other postcards.

I was a light-skinned Black woman, so the bruises showed up readily and clearly where he'd hurt me. With Jeurl's encouragement, I started to hide money in the hem of my skirt, and sometimes in the bun of my hair. Back then, these were skills that women possessed and passed down to each other. Some call it an act of bravery or resilience, but for us, it was as simple survival. Just like our grandmothers and their mothers braiding rice and seed into their hair and hemming coins into their clothing so they could escape slavery with a fresh start, I was stashing a little hope as well.

I would save small bills to trade into larger ones, and then I would hide them. If I didn't take those steps, Robert would take all my money and spend it on liquor. Once I collected enough money, I waited for him to go to work and then took a bus to Los

Angeles, California. I left clues for Robert about where I was headed, but that was part of a greater plan. Once I arrived in Los Angeles, I purchased another ticket to Gallup, New Mexico. While he searched for me in the city, I would be long gone with my Aunt Florence, my mother's sister, who gave me safe haven.

I never saw Robert again. He died in California of a heart attack as an alcoholic. I am not the type of person to wish bad on anybody or find pleasure in their misfortune, but learning this, somehow felt like a small token of justice in an otherwise unjust world. He was an abusive person, and I like to think God knows how to settle a score.

# 7

## Bartlesville

Robert missed the birth of our son, Ronald Ford Fletcher who was born in 1946 while I was still in Gallup, New Mexico. Aunt Florence was a tremendous help and I thank God for her and her wisdom. It was nice to be with her and around some family, but I longed for the people I called home. I wanted to return to Oklahoma. When I eventually regained my strength after the birth, I packed my few belongings, took my young son, and left Gallup.

After heavy consideration, I decided Bartlesville would be better than Tulsa. Even though it had been nearly twenty-five years since the massacre, it remained fresh to me, like a wound that refused to heal. Bartlesville, known for being the headquarters of Phillips Petroleum and Oil Company, was close enough and a place where I could plant new roots.

My older sister Jeurl was tormented by nightmares that continued to haunt her from Tulsa. They were always the same: the massacre, the blood, and a man being shot by a white man with a shotgun. I, too, was haunted by these same terrible memories. When I decided to move to Bartlesville after the war, instead of returning to Tulsa, Jeurl wanted to come with me and start anew. We ended up living on the same street, with our houses on opposite ends of the block. Our children played together and often stayed with each other. At one point, there were five families from our immediate family living on the same street.

Me with my son Ronald

A walk down the street felt like being in a village where each household played a role in raising the children. It was like having a community of grandparents, aunts, uncles, and cousins all on the same street. If any of the kids were up to something, someone was watching. We didn't have fancy technology like ring doorbells or Wi-Fi cameras, but we had something even better—big mommas sitting on the porch, keeping a watchful eye. They knew everyone's family history and could connect us all like a puzzle.

* * *

Everyone knew each other in our neighborhood which meant your personal business was always personal, but it was all in good fun. When someone needed help, a neighbor lent a hand. We didn't have social media or cell phones back then, so we had to rely on face-to-face communication. You'd simply walk down the street and knock on someone's door if someone needed to get in touch. And if you heard the phone ringing, you knew it was either a telemarketer or someone trying to sell something. But even then, we didn't mind the interruption. It was just part of life in our little community.

After Tulsa, we were wary of anyone who did not live on the street, especially if they were White. Word would spread quickly through the community if showed up who wasn't a resident of the area or if someone was up to no good. Phones would start ringing and people would share information about the person or company trying to sell something, like a Hoover vacuum cleaner. We had a neighborhood watch system but without the fancy technology of the modern day.

Bartlesville was a tight-knit community where we all looked out for one another.

We were all still in survival mode, dealing with the emotional trauma of the massacre and ongoing hostilities from Whites toward Blacks. This was only a few years before the brutal murder of Emmett Till and Black folks were regularly being lynched. We knew that looking after our own was essential to our survival, and that meant keeping our community safe and free from unwanted attention.

As a Black mother to boys, I was devastated when I heard about Emmett Till's lynching. It was like a punch to the gut, a reminder of the horrors we had experienced in Tulsa and continued to face in our everyday lives. To see a 14-year-old boy–a child not much older than my sons–so brutally tortured and murdered simply for being Black was heart-wrenching. I was reminded that no matter how much progress we had made, we were still not safe. Till's murder caused us to be more vigilant about protecting our families and communities.

The sad truth about the lynching of Emmett Till was that it was not surprising. It was shocking in the way that the murder of a child will always be, but we knew all too well what White people were capable of, and we had seen it play out time and time again. It did, however, reinforce the deep-seated mistrust and fear that many of us had for White people. We knew that not all White people were like those who had lynched Emmett Till, but generally, we also knew that we couldn't always trust them to have our best interests at heart.

The Emmett Till lynching was emotionally exasperating. It brought back memories I want to forget even now, a century later. We all wondered when the violence would end. Would we ever be truly safe? America still had a long way to go before claiming there was liberty and justice for all.

\* \* \*

A couple of years after moving to Bartlesville, I gave birth to my second child, James Edward Ford. I had to give birth in the basement of Jane Phillips Hospital near the hot water steam pipes because women of color were discriminated against at that hospital, just as we were in so many other places. Black women were not allowed to deliver their babies in the main portion of the hospital like White women. It reminded me of my brother Redd saying that during the war, Black soldiers on US ships could not sleep in the main quarters. They had to sleep five levels down in the hull.

I was accompanied by my mother and sister when I walked into Jane Phillips Hospital. I felt anxious but hopeful about the birth of my baby. The basement was a dismal and unsanitary place with concrete floors, little ventilation, cobwebs, and even rats and roaches. It was a small room that was already occupied by other women of color. The only available bed was next to the steam pipes, which made the room hot and uncomfortable.

As I lay there, I longed for the presence of my grandmother, who was a midwife and always knew how to bring me comfort. However, she could no longer work as a midwife because she had gone blind. Instead, I was attended to by two nurses with vastly different attitudes toward race. The first nurse was rough and uncaring, treating me and the other women with disdain. She seemed to take pleasure in our discomfort and did not provide adequate care.

The second nurse was a young white woman who seemed to genuinely care about her patients. She treated us with respect and empathy and was clearly frustrated by the discriminatory policies that forced us into the dingy basement. Her kindness was a beacon of hope in an otherwise bleak experience. This encounter made an impression on me, and I began to realize that the color of one's skin did not always dictate the content of their character.

Despite the challenges, my baby was delivered safely, and as soon as I was mentally ready, we left the hospital and received real care at home with the help of midwives. They made sure that everything was okay, including the umbilical cord, which was clamped off, and the removal of the placenta, which the hospital staff had refused to do.

* * *

I still remember the day I met James's father, Leroy Anderson. He was a charming and handsome Black man with big dreams and entrepreneurial ambitions. I was immediately impressed by his inventions. He reminded me of my father, who had saved our lives during the massacre.

Leroy was also a patriot and served in the war efforts, just like many of the other young men of our time. But his ambitions took him to Arizona, and he didn't know then that I was pregnant with his child. I was hesitant to tell him, fearing that he might not want to take on the responsibility of a child so far away. But eventually, I knew I had to.

When I finally told Leroy about his child, he promised to come back for me, but he didn't follow through. Instead, he found a new love in Arizona, got her pregnant, and built the large family he had always dreamed of. He had seven kids. It stung deeply. I felt betrayed by Leroy but I didn't let that consume me. I took the high ground and wished him well. I knew I had to move forward with my life, and Bartlesville became my home for the next seventy years.

So there I was, with two sons, James and Robert, to raise all on my own. The weight of the world seemed to rest on my shoulders as I navigated the challenges of being a single mother in a society that didn't always value or support Black women like me. Leroy's absence was a constant reminder of broken promises and shattered dreams, I struggled to make ends meet, working long hours and taking on any job I could find. There were days when I was exhausted to the bone, but I had no choice but to keep pushing forward for the sake of my children.

I watched my boys grow up without a father figure, and it pained me to see them yearn for a presence that wasn't there. In the end, I know that everything happens for a reason. If Leroy had stayed with me, things might have been different, but I wouldn't trade the life I have now for anything. I am grateful for the people and experiences that have shaped me into who I am today.

Through all of that hardship, my faith and the support of the Black community provided me with solace. The Four Leaf Clover Club and Starlight Baptist Church became my pillars of strength, where I found camaraderie and encouragement from fellow Black women who understood the struggles we faced. We shared stories, tears, and laughter, and we lifted each other when times were tough.

I remember the nights when I would stay up late, pouring over my bills and wondering how I would make ends meet. I tried to shield my children from my worries, putting on a brave face, but there were moments when I would break down in tears, feeling overwhelmed and alone. The weight of responsibility was heavy, and there were times when I doubted myself, wondering if I was doing enough for my children.

I refused to give up. I was determined to provide my sons with opportunities that I didn't have and to break the barriers that society tried to impose on us. I encouraged James and Ronald to dream big and pursue their passions, even when the odds seemed stacked against them. I cheered them on from the sidelines at their football games and school performances, and their smiles and achievements brought me immeasurable joy. As my sons grew older, I instilled in them the values of hard work, resilience, and perseverance. I encouraged their education and supported their dreams and aspirations. I wanted them to have opportunities that I never had, and I was determined to break the cycle of discrimination and limitations that I had faced.

With only a fourth-grade education, I taught myself to read and write, and nobody knew about my limited schooling. Whenever I came across words or phrases I didn't understand, I would look them up in the dictionary or read Farmer's Almanac. I made sure to dress well, often receiving hand-me-down clothes from some of the wealthiest White families in Bartlesville whose homes I cleaned. I would also enjoy hunting for treasures at thrift stores, where I found fine things for myself and my children, including clothes donated by affluent White families.

I worked as a housemaid which meant having numerous and demanding responsibilities. I woke up early in the morning to start my chores and often worked late into the night to make sure everything was done properly. My daily tasks included doing laundry, ironing clothes, cooking meals for the family, and cleaning the entire house. I made sure every room was spotless, from the living room to the bedrooms, and that every surface was clean. Laundry was time-consuming as well, from sorting the clothes, washing them, drying them, and then ironing them. Cooking was perhaps the most challenging part of my job. I had to plan menus, shop for groceries, and then prepare and serve meals while ensuring that the kitchen was always clean and tidy.

I was not only responsible for the household chores but also became a counselor and friend to the wives of the families I worked for. Despite living in luxurious homes and having all the money in the world, these wives were not always happy. I spent countless hours listening to their problems, providing comfort, and good Christian advice when needed. These women lived privileged lives, but it was not always a bed of roses for them. They had their own set of challenges, from struggling to keep up with social expectations to dealing with infidelity in their marriages. I learned that being rich did not make a person happy. It just confirmed that true happiness comes from within and peace come from God.

And it was not just the wives who needed attention. Most often it was the children. The children were always underfoot, and I had to keep an eye on them to ensure their safety. I helped them with their homework, played games with them, and listened to their stories. I grew close to the children, and they often confided in me about their problems too. I remember one time when the youngest daughter came to me crying because she had lost her favorite toy. I comforted her and helped her search for the toy until we found it. Moments like these made me feel like more than just a housemaid; I was a counselor, a friend, and a mother figure.

This experience helped me that hatred was not something we're born with. It had to be taught and learned. Societal pressures made people grow up to believe certain things, but the reality was that we aren't all so different. Although these children lived differently than me and my family, they still needed someone to be kind to them and love them.

As the children grew older, I noticed a change in their behavior toward me. They became more self-conscious about being seen with a Black woman, especially in public. I remember the days when I used to drop them off at school, and they would run out of the car and into the building as if they were afraid of being seen with me.

It was difficult for me to see them behave that way, but I understood the pressure they felt to conform to society's expectations. I didn't hold it against them, and I continued to treat them with the same love and care that I always had. At home, they were still warm and friendly with me, and we enjoyed spending time together.

I knew that as they grew older, they would continue to face challenges that I couldn't help them with. Besides, I still had my own children. Still, I hoped that the lessons I had taught them would stay with them. I wanted them to remember that kindness, respect, and compassion were more important than social status or wealth.

Around this time, I met Alzena Stein, a real Black cowboy who participated in rodeos and possessed skills like breaking a horse, roping a steer on the run, and riding a bull. Alzena was originally from Austin, Texas. He was exciting, daring, and bold, like the real-life lone ranger (who was a Black man). He filled a void in my life that had been left by Leroy Anderson.

And then, a little bundle of joy arrived—my daughter and youngest child, Debra Stein Ford. Her arrival brought a renewed sense of purpose and motivation. I knew that I had to keep pushing forward, not just for my sons, but also for my daughter. I wanted to show her that a Black woman could overcome any obstacle and create a life of dignity and success.

However, tragedy struck Alzena. He had both of his legs amputated and eventually succumbed to cancer. Despite his untimely death, Alzena had faithfully provided support for his daughter before his passing, and even after his death, his military benefits continued to come in for a short while. But just five months later, the well ran dry, and I found myself back at square one. Once again, I was a single mother with no other support for my three children, except for what I earned as a housemaid.

My youngest daughter Debra

As many women know, being a single mother and playing the roles of both mother and father can be hard work. My relationships with men did not pan out fairly, and I had my share of challenges. After Alzena died, I decided to just stay focused on hard work and dedicated myself completely to being a good mother and raising my three children. As I watched them grow up into strong and independent individuals, I felt a swell of pride in my heart. They were my greatest achievement.

As I remember my children, it hurts because I have outlived two of them. No mother wants to say that. I lost my son James to cancer and my daughter Debra to congestive heart failure, leaving a gaping hole in my heart. It's hard to bear the grief of losing my flesh and blood. It's a wound that never fully heals.

My son James was a brave veteran who served his country, but he was exposed to toxic substances during his military service. When he filed for disability benefits, we found out his medical records were lost in a fire. It was frustrating and overwhelming trying to prove his disability, and he was only granted partial disability for anxiety. It was unfair and added to our family's pain.

My children were taken from me too soon, and their absence is felt every day. Amidst the darkness, I find solace in knowing their memories live on in me and that the Lord has them now. He is my comfort in all of this.

I also found joy in spending time with my grandchildren. As their grandmother, it was important to me that I instilled in them the values that I held dear, such as perseverance, hard work, and integrity. You see, coming from Black Wall Street, where your reputation was everything. You were only as good as your name and your word.

I taught my grandchildren that hard work and determination were essential to success. I encouraged them to pursue their dreams and never give up, even when times were tough. I reminded them that life was not always fair, but that didn't mean they couldn't overcome any obstacles in their way. No matter what life throws at you, you can always make lemonade out of lemons. I also taught them about the importance of integrity. I told them that if they gave their word, they must keep it and that they must be time-conscious. I made sure they understood that their reputation and credibility were important and could take a lifetime to build but only a moment to destroy. I showed my grandchildren that even if they had one pair of pants, they could wash and iron them to look like the best pair they ever had. And if there was a hole in the knee, we patched it up.

I remember when I had to teach my grandson about the importance of honesty and how to solve problems without compromising your principles. Ike was always a good boy, but like most young men, he had his fair share of admirers. One day, while we were sitting in the living room, the telephone rang. I answered. It was one of his girlfriends, and she wanted to speak to him.

I covered the mouth of the phone and told him to come get it. Ike was hesitant to answer. He told me to say he wasn't home, but I wasn't going to lie.

"Boy, come get this damn phone! I'm not going to lie for you," I said to him.

He didn't seem too happy with my response, but I knew I had to stick to my principles. I always believed that there's no need to lie. There's always a way to say something in a manner that doesn't make you a liar. After a little back and forth, Ike finally agreed to take the call. But he still didn't want to speak to the girl. So, I told him to step outside the door. Once he did, I moved my hand and told the girl he had just stepped outside.

When the call was over, I hung up the phone and Ike came back inside. I could see the relief on his face. I wanted to make sure that my grandson learned the importance of honesty and truthfulness. And that day, he learned that there are always ways to solve problems without resorting to lies.

* * *

I can't help but feel a mix of emotions – sorrow, love, and admiration – when thinking of my children. Their struggles and their unwavering spirits bring longing and pride. Their stories deserve to be shared, as much as mine. I wonder how their lives would be different if our family could have afforded adequate care. What might have become of my son if he (and his many Black brothers-in-arms) were able to receive their benefits? In a way, the same racism that took my future when I was a frightened child, fleeing a firestorm is the same mechanism at work here, still taking from me.

I continued working as a maid in rich, white households there in Bartlesville. One of those households was the Colemans. They didn't have any children. I washed their clothes and cleaned every room in the house. I also worked for the Price family, who did have children. They were the original owners of the Price Tower in Bartlesville, Oklahoma, designed by the famous Frank Lloyd Wright and constructed in 1952. I took their kids to school, field trips, and shopping, and yes, I cleaned the whole house.

The couple would soon have marital problems and I soon found myself with just one job instead of three, after they broke up. I then had to work temp cleaning jobs I got based on recommendations people made from my hard work for others. I would get down on my hands and knees to clean the floor. That's how you do it, right? I continued to work for the wealthy Coleman family for fifteen years. Old man Coleman even wrote me into his will; however, I would never see one red cent from that will. Mrs. Coleman saw to that. She insisted that she would have to die before I would receive anything from her husband's will. Mrs. Coleman did eventually pass, but I still never saw a dime.

The fact that I wasn't educated allowed these rich families to take advantage of me and skirt around the system. I tried not to let anything hold me back, but there was always a part of me that begrudged having my education stolen in the massacre. The shipyard was the only place that treated me fairly as a worker, once that was gone, so was the dignity of a fair wage and proper reporting.

I was often paid under the table, which in that way meant they didn't have to pay into my social security account. They made me believe that they were doing so, but I later discovered, too late, that they were not. It became clear to me much later that an employer's contributions to one's social security account would have a direct impact on their quality of life or lack thereof. Once I learned that important lesson, I made sure future employers who wanted my hard-working maid services did the right thing as far as government paperwork was concerned.

This injustice of employers not paying into my social security forced me to work until I was well into my eighties. I'm now 108 years of age and only stopped working at 85 because my back and knees were breaking down from so many years of scrubbing floors on my hands and knees. My first social security check was about $290.00. Imagine living on $290.00 a month at 85. I thank God every day that I have loving, grown-up grandchildren, who care and look out for me. They are the light I hold on to.

My sons
James and Ronald

My daughter
Debra

# PART III

# Justice Will Come

## 8

# A Tipping Point

I've lived a long hard life. Much of it has gone by without apology, acknowledgment, or attempts to make things right for any of us who escaped Tulsa that night 100 years ago. One hundred years is a long time to wait, a long time to live silently unrecognized while still carrying the burdens. But amidst the struggles and the scars, there have been some wonderful highlights. I am amazed at the turn of events in the last few years. It's been a remarkable chapter in my life, one that I never expected, but one that has given me renewed purpose and hope. To think, after all of that I, Viola Ford Fletcher, would sit before Congress to tell the whole world the truth.

I was filled with joy and amazement when my attorney, Damario Solomon Simmons, informed me that I had been invited to testify on the Tulsa Massacre at a Congressional Subcommittee, led by Rep. Sheila Jackson-Lee of Texas. I would be testifying alongside my only surviving brother, Redd, and Mother Lessie Randle, another survivor of that horrible night.

As I entered the majestic Capitol building and met the polite subcommittee members, I felt a mixture of nerves and determination. It was my first time speaking before a major government agency, and I was honored to represent my family and all the lost souls who came before me, particularly those who were murdered during the massacre and never had anyone to speak on their behalf. Despite feeling a sense of responsibility, I remained a strong woman and did not let intimidation overcome me. Here is my complete testimony from that day:

*My name is Viola Ford Fletcher, or Mother Fletcher. I am the daughter of Lucinda Ellis and John Wesley Ford of Tulsa, Oklahoma. I am the sister of Hughes Van Ellis, who is also here today. And I am a survivor of the Tulsa Race Massacre.*

*Two weeks ago, I celebrated my 107th birthday. Today, I am in Washington, D.C. for the first time in my life. I am here seeking justice. I am here asking my country to acknowledge what happened in Tulsa*

*in 1921. On May 31st, 1921, I went to bed in my family's home in the Greenwood neighborhood of Tulsa. The neighborhood I fell asleep in that night was rich – not just in terms of wealth, but in culture, community, and heritage. My family had a beautiful home. We had great neighbors and I had friends to play with. I felt safe. I had everything a child could need. I had a bright future ahead of me. Greenwood could have given me the chance to truly make it in this country. Within a few hours, all of that was gone.*

*The night of the Massacre I was woken up by my family. My parents and five siblings were there. I was told we had to leave.*

*And that was it. I will never forget the violence of the relentless, racist White mob when we left our house. I still see Black men being shot, and Black bodies lying in the street. I still smell smoke and see fire. I still see Black businesses being burned. I still hear airplanes flying overhead. I hear the screams. I live through the Massacre every day. Our country may forget this history. I cannot. I will not. The other survivors do not. And our descendants do not.*

*When my family was forced to leave Tulsa, I lost my chance at an education. I never finished school past the fourth grade. I have never made much money.*

*My country, state, and city took a lot from me. Despite this, I spent time supporting the war effort in the shipyards of California. But for most of my life, I was a domestic worker serving White families. I never made much money. To this day, I can barely afford my everyday needs. All the while the City of Tulsa has unjustly used the names and stories of victims like me to enrich itself and its White allies through the $30 million raised by the Tulsa Centennial Commission while I continue to live in poverty.*

*I am 107 years old and have never seen justice. I pray that one day I will. I have been blessed with a long life – and have seen the best and worst of this country. I think about the horrors inflicted upon Black people in this country every day. This subcommittee has the power to lead us down a better path. I am asking that my country acknowledge what has happened to me. The trauma. The pain. The loss. And I ask that survivors and descendants be given a chance to seek justice. Open the courtroom doors to us. I believe we must acknowledge America's sins. It is the least we can do. I saw what happened here on January 6th this year. It broke my heart. It reminded me of what happened 100 years ago. And now, I hear some of you on TV saying it didn't happen, like we didn't see it with our own eyes. It happened on live TV.*

*One-hundred years ago, there was no TV, but you have me here right now. You see Mother Randle. You see my brother, Hughes Van Ellis. We lived this history. We can't ignore it. It lives with us. We lost everything that day. Our homes. Our churches. Our newspapers. Our theaters. Our lives.*

*Greenwood represented the best of what was possible for Black people in America – and for all people. No one cared about us for almost 100 years. We, and our history, have been forgotten, washed away. This Congress must recognize us, and our history -- for Black*

*Americans, for the White Americans, and for all Americans. That is some justice.*

My brother Redd Spoke after me. As moved as the members of the Congressional subcommittee were by my testimony, I had only warmed up the audience. His testimony, which opened this book, stole the show.

My baby brother, now a centennial like me, spoke truthfully and with clarity to the whole room. He held them accountable to the promise of the nation we have served in many ways for over 100 years. He reminded everyone, that we are truly one nation under God, and it was time to right what was wrong. I could not have been more proud of my family.

When he finished speaking, it was evident that his message was heard. He was given a standing ovation. My grandson told me afterward that there was not a dry eye in the room. So perhaps America does have a conscience.

But what would this committee do? It did not take long to get our answer.

Shortly after testifying, Congresswoman Sheila Jackson Lee visited us at our hotel. She had been our advocate and defender through this entire ordeal, a service for which my whole family is grateful. She presented us with House Resolution 215 (H.Res.215). This resolution officially acknowledges what happened to us – an act of pure and bitter hatred that killed hundreds and left thousands homeless and unable to recover.

Was this Justice? Almost. It was a step in that direction.

Since that great opportunity to speak my peace in the U.S. Capitol Building, I've been inundated with requests by national news media for personal interviews. So much interest in telling the true story of the biggest racial massacre in US history, even President Joe Biden came to see me, my family, Mother Randle, and my brother Redd. I was honored to meet him and to know that the President of the United States wanted to hear from me. He also told me that: "What happened in Tulsa in 1921, was the first time in the history of the United States that American citizens dropped bombs on other Americans...."

I was later told that this would be the first time a sitting Democratic president flew Air Force One to the red state of Oklahoma in 100 years. As we gathered to listen to the President's news conference following our private visit, I was greeted by Rev. Jesse Jackson, Rev. Al Sharpton, and star civil rights attorney Ben

Crump, who had stood up for the George Floyd family in the aftermath of his brutal murder by police. We met them all, and they were so pleased to chat and take photographs with Redd and me.

For a moment, I felt like one of the movie stars I always see on TV. Calls were now coming in from NBC, CBS, ABC, and CNN. I was told that there were two new documentary films airing on TV that were made to commemorate the centennial of the Tulsa Race Massacre. One of those films was executive produced by LeBron James and his then-teammate Russell Westbrook, and I thought it was so nice to see young, wealthy Black athletes using their platform and resources to educate our people. Mother Randle and I even made our way into the world of hip-hop when we did a Zoom call with Jay-Z. I'm not familiar with his work, but I know for a fact he has a beautiful wife and that he is an established young businessman who is doing us proud.

Finally, the American public of the twenty-first century wanted to know more about a terrible episode that had either been whitewashed or eliminated from the history books. But the facts concerning those events were never far from my mind. Never. In fact, for every day, for 100 years, I've found it nearly impossible to enjoy a good night's sleep. Some terrified place in me relives the horror of that first night of the massacre every damn night. I cannot sleep in a bed, remembering how our mother came running into our bedroom calling for Jeurl and me to gather up whatever we could because we had to leave the house immediately. She said, "There were White people outside killing Black people! I was only seven years old at the time, and I'm 108 years old now. Imagine having the same horrible nightmare every night for 100 years.

But I received another wonderful surprise around the time of Tulsa, Oklahoma's Juneteenth celebration, where Redd and I were honorary parade marshals and guests of the Justice for Greenwood organization that coordinated the festivities. The streets were lined with so many people as Redd and I were presented in a horse-drawn carriage, draped with a Kente cloth blanket gifted by a supporter from New York City. The Tulsa Race Massacre centennial commemoration was another special occasion that garnered national attention. We were celebrated at several receptions and interviewed by reporters from prominent newspapers like The Washington Post and local stations, as well as networks.

Throughout the commemorative events, we had the pleasure of meeting two extraordinary young Black men, Michael Thompson and his brother Eric, who had traveled from the Washington, DC area to Tulsa. They had created something wonderful, an online social media business called Our Black Truth. Michael Thompson passionately explained to me what their business intended to do for Black folks, and I was inspired by their vision. It reminded me of the importance of African Americans coming together to tell our story, just as I had done on Capitol Hill when I testified there in May of 2021.

Michael asked me about something I had always wanted to do but hadn't yet had the chance. Immediately, my mind drifted back to that moment when I was lying in a wheat field and saw a cloud shaped like an elephant. Without hesitation, I blurted out that I wanted to see Africa and the pyramids of Egypt and to meet real live African people. I knew that our history in this country traced back to Africa, the cradle of civilization, and I had always hoped to visit there "before I caught my wings" and flew to Heaven. To my amazement, I saw Michael's eyes light up as he smiled and said, "I'm going to make that happen, ma'am!"

I could hardly believe it. I was actually going to see Africa! I knew that whatever lay ahead was going to be the journey of a lifetime.

# 9

# A Dream Come True

Michael Thompson kept his promise and made arrangements for me to travel to Africa. Not only that, but he also included my beloved brother, Redd, who I always wanted by my side for big moments, and even some of our family members who are descendants of the massacre survivors. It was unbelievable! A century after the worst race massacre in American history, that little girl and her only surviving sibling are going to Africa.

Originally, I had asked to also go to Egypt to see the pyramids, as Egypt is also in Africa. I had always considered it the crown jewel of ancient civilizations, and I had taught myself to read just so I could learn more about ancient Egypt. However, the folks at Our Black Truth had only committed to taking us to West Africa and Ghana, and that was more than enough for me. They were concerned about my age and the long flight across the world to Egypt and then back to West Africa to Accra, Ghana. It was during this time that I learned that Africa was a continent, and one so vast that you could fit many other nations inside it, like a jigsaw puzzle. You could fit the whole United States, France, Russia, China, and all of Europe inside the African continent and still have room for more. It was an astonishing fact.

The preparations for the trip felt like moving an army unit. Everyone had to have their Covid-19 vaccinations, as we were traveling internationally during the pandemic, and Ghana had strict passport regulations. We also had to get yellow fever shots to protect against mosquitos. Most of the world was quarantined because they were afraid of the virus, but I wanted to see Africa.

I realized I needed some new clothes too. Despite being 108 years old, I still had a woman's sense of vanity and wanted to present myself well in public. I had always taken pride in making a good appearance, but when we escaped the massacre, all I had with me were the clothes on my back and a few things I could grab as we made our way to the wagon Daddy was hitching up.

Over the years, I accumulated some nice clothes, especially while working as a maid. The families I worked for would sometimes give me their old clothes. Most of the time, the garments were meant to be thrown away, but I would take them home and fix them up. Nothing went to waste. Good material was always repurposed. I would often use the fabric from old dresses and skirts to make blouses or turn a worn-out jacket into a new cardigan. And if the clothes were already in good condition, I would wear them proudly. Nice clothes made me feel like I was worth something, even if the world around me sometimes treated me otherwise.

Now that I was going to Africa, I wanted to look my best. My grandkids helped me buy some new clothes for the trip. Redd had also found some nice things for himself. He had been in the military, and all the military men from those days after World War II were quite sharp and handsome. My brother Redd was no exception with his sharp features and light reddish-brown complexion that earned him the nickname "Redd." He looked very striking by the time we left.

During the preparations, our close family friend, Oklahoma State Representative Regina Goodwin had been helping my grandson Ike with facilitating many of the media requests coming in from Mr. Tony Regusters, the international spokesperson for Our Black Truth. They arranged a couple of interviews with the Black American news media and The Washington Post newspaper. Rep. Goodwin also organized and presided over a press conference in Tulsa as a send-off for our upcoming trip to Ghana. A media campaign was launched to let the public know that Redd and I, along with many of our descendants, would soon be on our way to Ghana. I did a few interviews by myself, and an executive from Our Black Truth did several interviews for TV, newspapers, and radio. She even did a few interviews alongside me.

There was immense interest in the story of a 107-year-old Black woman and her younger 100-year-old brother, who had survived the Tulsa Race Massacre of 1921 and were now going to Africa. Mother Lessie Randle and I had lived long enough to tell the tale and speak for the dead and forgotten. Michael Thompson of Our Black Truth had aptly called it "Coming Home: The Journey of a Lifetime." We had a conference call with Ambassador Dr. Erieka Bennett, founder, and head of Mission of the Diaspora African Forum, who told us that the people of Ghana were thrilled about our visit. We owe her a lot of gratitude because she was one of the main coordinators who made our trip possible.

Our itinerary consisted of meeting dignitaries, including Ghana's head-of-state, President Nana Akufo-Adoo. We were to be celebrated by a wealthy Chief from Nigeria living in Ghana, visit the grave and memorial of Dr. W.E.B. DuBois, and see the dungeon where enslaved people were kept before being sent to the Caribbean and the United States. Interviews on Ghanaian TV were also lined up. But what excited me the most was the prospect of meeting the actual people of Ghana.

Before leaving Tulsa (Redd was living in Denver, Colorado, and would fly from there), we saw photographs of the resort hotel where we would be staying, the La Palm Royal Beach Hotel, situated on the shores of the Atlantic Ocean. The same ocean that our stolen and brutalized ancestors had crossed during the transatlantic slave trade.

As our travel arrangements were being finalized, I imagined what it would be like to set foot in Africa and see the rising sun of Africa on that first morning. I wondered if my ancestors would know that I had returned, if Granny Dora Love and my mother would look down from the heavens and see me, Redd, and our families there. My grandson drove from Dallas to Tulsa a week before the trip because I was being hospitalized with fluid around my heart, feeling as if someone was trying to smother me with an invisible pillow. I experienced chest pains and severe anxiety, especially considering that my older sister Jeurl had died of congestive heart failure. I had never been treated in a proper hospital before. After all, I had given birth to two of my children in the basement of a hospital in Bartlesville, lying near a hot water pipe as though I wasn't a human being. But now, in 2021, the hospital staff had me hooked up to all these modern machines and computers to monitor my vital signs. They even served me breakfast in bed!

I was afraid that my health condition would prevent me from realizing this long-awaited dream, but my grandson Ike always told me, "Granny, it's mind over matter. If you don't move it, you lose it!" So, I immediately changed my mindset and was determined not to let anything hold me back. When Ike arrived from Texas, he explained the purpose of all the equipment and even taught me how to use the remote to change TV channels. He was such a loving grandson, sleeping on the couch in my room until the doctors and nurses at Tulsa's St. Francis Hospital gave me a clean bill of health. I was now ready to travel to Ghana.

I think every African American should take at least one trip to Africa in their lifetime. Amidst health conditions, old age, and a global pandemic I still made it. And if I could do it, what is your excuse? I hope my story serves as an inspiration for others to push past their own limitations and pursue their dreams, no matter how big or small they may seem.

* * *

The moment had finally arrived. My grandson, Ike, drove me down to Dallas, and we flew out of Dallas-Fort Worth International Airport to meet up with Redd and others at New York's John F. Kennedy International Airport (JFK) in New York. Then we arrived at JFK, where we were warmly greeted by Redd, Michael Thompson, and other family members who were joining us on the journey. We were treated with the utmost respect, ushered into the VIP lounge, and made to feel like diplomats. With our flight time drawing near, I could barely contain my excitement; I was ready to go. Soon enough, we boarded the plane for a 10-hour flight to Ghana.

Our flight was scheduled for 11:00 pm, which meant we would arrive in Ghana the next morning. Redd and I were fortunate to have seats in the business class, just a few steps away from the restrooms. The seats were incredibly comfortable, assuring us of a smooth flight. At 107 years of age, a 10-hour flight could feel quite long, but I was eager and willing to make the journey. As the plane took off and accelerated down the runway, I felt the awe-inspiring power of the aircraft. It was a thrilling experience. I also couldn't help but notice that most of the flight attendants were African American, which made me feel incredibly proud.

Ever since the night of the massacre, I have been unable to sleep in a bed. I have always slept in a chair, usually with the lights on. Part of me is always anxious about something like that happening again. I've always believed if people could be brazen enough to do it once, they could do it again. Also, when I sleep, it is never very deep or for very long because of the anxiety and the things I see. When you go through so much hardship, your experiences stay with you. Despite the trauma, I found some comfort in the familiar confines of an airline seat, allowing me to doze off for at least three hours.

As I reflect on my struggles with sleep, I am reminded of how my siblings and other family members have also suffered due to the trauma inflicted by the massacre.

My older sister, Jeurl Ishem, who lived near me in Bartlesville, Oklahoma, experienced a heart condition that required her to need a pacemaker. Jeurl, a devout Christian who led a simple life and never learned to drive, was part of the loving and well-known Ishem family in Bartlesville. It pains me deeply to think about the profound loss I felt when Jeurl passed away due to excess fluid in her lungs.

My brother John, who lived in California, struggled to recover from the traumatic events of the massacre. He turned to heavy drinking as a way to cope, consuming a full bottle of Vodka every day. Tragically, he passed away in a nursing home due to cirrhosis of the liver.

My brother Cleon

Cleon, who worked as an independent trash collector in our adopted hometown of Bartlesville, also suffered greatly. He had a stroke and heart attack that eventually took his life. Like John, Cleon was also a heavy drinker, and I believe it was his way of coping with the aftermath of the massacre and our family's troubles. Today, we would call it PTSD.

Sarah, who lived through the turmoil we experienced as a family on the run, also faced her own challenges. She lost her ability to function mentally and required constant care. She has also passed away and is laid to rest in Bartlesville's White Rose Cemetery, alongside Cleon, Jeurl, and our mother, Lucinda Ellis.

My brother Albert, who fought in World War II and was exposed to a chemical agent, experienced severe physical problems that eventually led to kidney failure. He passed away while on dialysis, and there was no hero's welcome for Black men like him, who fought for a country that denied them the honors they deserved. Mary, my sweet baby sister and twin to my brother Albert, died at the tender age of two. In my spiritual mind, I believe she will be the first person in my family to greet me when I finally catch my wings.

Time passed, and soon we were closing in on Africa. I could almost feel the Motherland calling out to me from mid-air. When we landed at Ghana's Kotoka International Airport, we disembarked and were warmly greeted by Ambassador Erieka Bennett and Rev. Toni Luck, who had been working with Our Black Truth to organize our trip. We underwent Covid-19 tests at the airport's diplomatic lounge, and once cleared, Ambassador Bennett led us to a Mercedes-Benz that would take us to our hotel.

We had ample security and a police escort with sirens blaring as we made our way through the streets of Accra to our hotel. When we arrived at the La Palm Royal Beach Hotel, we were greeted by an African ensemble of dancers and drummers. It was exhilarating to be welcomed in such a special way. We were escorted into the hotel lobby, where a singer performed a song called "Welcome Home." It was deeply moving. Our suites were well-stocked with fresh fruits, flowers, and custom-made African garments in our closets, courtesy of Ambassador Bennett's staff. I was grateful for it all, including the helpful staff at the La Palm Hotel, who were kind and accommodating.

We rested for a while and were later guided to the hotel conference room to discuss the itinerary for the days ahead, including an opportunity to exchange American dollars for Ghana's currency. That evening, at the La Palm's ocean-side restaurant, we enjoyed a buffet-style dinner with music and dancing, surrounded by family and guests. As we sat there by the ocean, listening to the rhythmic waves crashing on the shoreline, I experienced what I can only describe as a spiritual awakening. It felt as though my ancestors were whispering, "Welcome Home..." and Redd and I truly felt accepted and comforted by Ghana's warm embrace.

Front row standing: **Rabbi Kohain Halevi Nathanyah**, Executive Director PANAFEST Foundation, Dr. Ambassador **Erieka Bennett**, Founder D.A.F, **Ike Howard**, President/CEO Viola Ford Fletcher Foundation, **H.E. Nana Akufo Addo**, President of Ghana, **Muriel Ellis** and **Malee Vivian Craft**, daughters of Uncle Redd, **Dr. Toni Luck** and Chief of Staff at the Office of the President, **Frema Opare**. Back row standing: Director of Diaspora Affairs, **Akwasi Ababio**, Deputy Minister of Tourism, Arts and Culture, **Mark Okraku-Mantey**, Minister of Tourism, Arts and Culture, **Dr. Ibrahim Awal**, Chairman and President of OBT Social, **Michael A. Thompson**, Deputy Director Diaspora Affairs, Office of the President, **Dr. Nadia Musa**.

\* \* \*

Redd and I, along with our family members, spent the rest of our first day in Ghana resting after our long overnight journey across the Atlantic. The following day was Sunday, and our itinerary included a service at the Action Chapel Church in Accra. The church was a mega-church in Africa, presided over by Archbishop Nicholas Duncan-Williams, who had left a video-recorded message to welcome us as he was traveling at that time. The service was led by his first lady, Mrs. Rosa Whitaker-Williams, a former Assistant US Trade Representative for Africa in the administrations of US Presidents Bill Clinton and George W. Bush.

The Action Chapel Church service was truly beautiful, with a massive congregation in attendance. As we entered, Redd and I were given a standing ovation. Mrs. Rosa Whitaker was a very impressive and welcoming host, and despite feeling a bit tired from our overnight flight, I couldn't help but be energized by the beautiful voices of the Action Chapel choir. After the church service, we took a photograph with the congregation and our family members surrounding us.

We then proceeded to a lovely luncheon, and afterward, I participated in a video-recorded interview on a stage at the church with Mrs. Rosa Whitaker. Over the next few days, my grandson Ike, Michael Thompson of Our Black Truth, and Ambassador Bennett conducted numerous interviews with Ghanaian and other African news media. It was thrilling to see stories about our visit appearing on Accra's television stations and in newspapers. It seemed that people were amazed by my sharp mind at the age of 108. The excitement around Redd and me was palpable everywhere we went.

The honors and events continued to unfold at a whirlwind pace. Everything was meticulously coordinated, from security to transportation. We were even provided with specially made clothing for each event on our itinerary. We traveled in a convoy, with a big bus full of media, three motorcycles to navigate traffic, a security vehicle with national police, and private cars. Our every move was facilitated with on-site police sirens and lights to ensure we could travel seamlessly from point A to point B. We had the opportunity to experience African cuisine, visiting a restaurant called Asmara that offered a variety of African dishes.

One of the highlights was an ambassadors' tea event held in our honor at the La Palm Hotel, where we were presented with a booklet containing a special welcome from the Dean of the Diplomatic Corps in Ghana, Ambassador Claudia Turbay Quintero. She is the ambassador of Colombia to Ghana. Her welcome statement from the booklet read: *On behalf of the African Diplomatic Corps, I extend heartfelt greetings to these honored centenarians, Mother Viola Fletcher and Uncle Redd, who experienced the terrors of the 'Black Wall Street Massacre' as children at Tulsa, Oklahoma in 1921. It is our hope that this wonderful and unique experience, realizing the blessing of a dream come true, to see Africa in their remaining years, can be a balm to soothe those terrible memories. Welcome, Mrs. Fletcher, Mr. Van Ellis, and a delegation of family members, to the Motherland!*

One of the next things on my list of special events was an official meeting with an African king. He was His Royal Majesty, King Tackie Teiko Tsuru II, the Ga Manste, and I learned that he is married to a Ghanaian Supreme Court judge. He is also the President of the Ga Traditional Council and bestowed traditional Ga names on us. Mine is Naa Yaoteley Fletcher (which loosely translates to "Queen Mother"). The meeting was held outside of his mansion in a big white tent with butlers dressed in black tuxedo jackets and bowties wearing white gloves. Very fancy! Redd and I both received laminated certificates with our African names displayed on them.

Our next event was profoundly touching. It took place at the embassy of the Diaspora African Forum, where Redd and I unveiled plaques honoring our deceased immediate family members on the Sankofa Wall. "Sankofa" is a word from Ghana's Akan people meaning "remember where you came from, and don't forget to return." There is an ancient symbol for the saying that shows a bird flying forward but with its head turned backward.

The names Redd and I submitted for the plaques were the five deceased relatives we shared included: my son and Ike's father, James Edward Ford. Then there was my beloved older sister, Jeurl Ishem, and Redd's deceased wife Mabel Ellis, my wise and brave mother Lucinda Ellis, and my daughter Debra Stein Crumpton, who tragically died of congestive heart failure, just like my sister Jeurl did. We unveiled the plaques and poured some libation on the ground in their honor. The ceremony, attended by our family members and a large number of people from the news, was beautifully touching.

After the unveiling, walked a short distance from the elegant, white embassy building of the Diaspora African Forum and Sankofa Wall, across the campus of the W.E.B. DuBois Cultural Center to visit and pay homage to Dr. W.E.B. DuBois, whose body is interred there in a walk-in mausoleum.

* * *

Redd and I took part in a traditional Ibo ceremony and pageant called a "grand durbar" which was presided over by His Majesty Chukwudi Ihenetu, King of the Ibo community of Ghana. He extended such a warm and gracious greeting that it felt more like a blessing. Here are his beautiful words of welcome to Redd and me: "You are welcomed back to the ancestors' land – your continent where you come from. A continent filled with milk and honey! We are so PROUD to have you back in Africa! God bless you, may God give you more life, and may God strengthen you more, because we need you. Thank you. God bless you..."

The event was full of incredible dancing with men dressed in straw, wearing masks, and walking on stilts. We were spellbound by the amazing drumming, the food, everything. I felt as if we were transported back in time to another Africa, an Africa of the ancient world. And to top it off, King Ihenetu crowned me a "Queen Mother" and Redd was made a chief. My heart was now overflowing with joy and gratitude like that proverbial cup in the Bible.

The next day, Redd and I, along with our whole entourage, traveled to the Economic Community of West African States (ECOWAS) headquarters in the Osu area of Accra. Deep beneath the ground of one of the old buildings on the complex, right next to the Atlantic Ocean, there is a dungeon where kidnapped people were chained and jailed, and sent into the bellies of slave ships headed to the American colonies. Redd and I did not go down there, but the younger people traveling with us did.

I, along with Ambassador Bennett and Dr. Toni Luck, watched from a high balcony as the younger people went from the dungeon to the beach where they were given flowers which they threw into the ocean with prayers for lost ancestors. When Ambassador Bennett told us about how the people in that dungeon and others in Ghana, Senegal, and other places were treated, Redd asked, "What kind of people would do such a thing? Enslave free people and force inhumane conditions on them?" Dr. Toni Luck turned to Redd and gave him the answer: "The same kind of people that destroyed the prosperous Black community in Tulsa, Oklahoma..."

One of our final visits of this "Journey of a Lifetime" was with the President of Ghana, His Excellency Nana Akufo-Addo. The meeting took place in a conference room at the Golden Jubilee House, their version of our White House. The president was very gracious and expressed many kind words of welcome. He also understood how much Black people in the United States had suffered, not only during slavery but also since then.

There was an opportunity when we returned to the hotel for anyone who wanted to travel with a guide, round-trip on a tour bus to the Cape Coast region to see a real slave castle, which I understood to be far worse than the one we saw in Accra. Some of the young women in our group took the opportunity to make the trip. When they returned, every one of them looked shaken as if they had all seen a ghost. They spoke about feeling the terrified spirits of the ancestors who were imprisoned in those dungeons until they were sold and then shipped off across the ocean to a life of enslavement – if they survived the journey.

Redd and I received so many honors received and visited so many wonderful places, that my head was swirling with pride and joy from all the loving treatment by the people of Ghana.

The evening before we would be returning to the United States, a farewell dinner was held in our honor at Ambassador Bennett's home. When we returned to the hotel, I got one last look at the ocean and I imagined what it must have been like inside the belly of a slave ship for months on end and then endure centuries of enslavement and Jim Crow Era terror and oppression. I sent a prayer across the ocean for all of us, that we may never have to endure days like that ever again.

## 10

# A Day in Court

September 28, 2021

My grandson wheeled me into the courtroom for the preliminary hearing around 10 a.m. We changed courtrooms for one much larger because there were so many people. It appeared to me that there were about twenty to twenty-five different lawyers in the courtroom. I sat patiently with the other two Greenwood survivors, Redd and Mother Randle. We were all anxious.

Even though we had testified before Congress to tell our stories from that night, we were together again watching our legal team defend our "public nuisance" lawsuit in a Tulsa court. If successful, the lawsuit would go to trial, and if successful at trial, the state would officially recognize the massacre as a public nuisance for how it has harmed the Black community of Tulsa for decades. This would open the door wider to receive some form of restitution for the survivors and their families.

Attempts were made to dismiss the case entirely. While we

know what side of history we were on, some wanted to see the case thrown out before it went to trial.

Our lawyer Damario contacted my family and me shortly after my 106th birthday celebration. He was working on efforts to bring restoration and justice to the Greenwood community, something that no one else has been able to do in my long lifetime. At first, I was not sure I wanted to be a part of whatever he was doing. I had lived all of my life without getting even so much as an apology; I did not need to relive the pain or get my hopes up. I did not want to put my face in front of the world. Everyone else around me had failed and passed on without so much as a day in court. My grandson Ike reminded me that it is important to tell my story because I deserved to be known and remembered properly. He did not want to see them rewrite me into a false version of history, and he told me not to let them bury my story.

So there I was, in a courtroom, with my brother, Mother Randle, and a whole team of lawyers from around the country. Together, we were pushing for whatever it took to replace what we lost. This was to include a formal acknowledgment of the pain that was caused and the truth of what was done to our community. It also meant repayment of the damages so that we could create the opportunities our children and their children could have had if we had been allowed to live our lives. We wanted to see these benefits come to pass in our lifetime. None of us really knew what was to come of it, but I knew God always has a way to make things right in his time.

Soon, the judge came in and set the tone for the proceedings. The arguments lasted until about 6:00 p.m. Our lead attorney, Damario, had prepared a detailed slide show presentation that clearly outlined why our lawsuit against the city of Tulsa should move forward. Now it was up to the judge to weigh the many arguments. As I sat in court, I couldn't help but think back to the incident that sparked the massacre – a Black man being falsely accused of accosting a White woman.

When the judge dismissed the court, I returned from my daydream and the memories that have haunted me for so long. As with all things, I placed whatever would be in the hands of Almighty God. He would bring justice and atonement for those crimes.

In 2023, we finally saw a glimmer of hope in our pursuit of true justice. A judge in Tulsa gave us the green light to proceed to trial. It's not a guarantee of victory, but it's the first real chance we've had in all these years.

We're now filled with a renewed sense of determination. We know it won't be easy. The scars of the past are still fresh, and the wounds are far from healed. But we're ready to take this step forward, just like our ancestors who fought for their rights and dignity.

We are seeking justice, not just for ourselves, but for all those who suffered in silence, for the lives lost, for the dreams shattered, and for the generations that have been denied the truth for far too long. This trial is just the beginning, and we know there are no guarantees of victory. But for the first time in a century, we have a chance to make our voices heard in a court of law, to demand accountability, and to seek redress for the wrongs that have been done.

I feel a renewed sense of hope as I stand on the threshold of this historic moment. I believe that justice is possible, and I'm determined to see it through. We may have waited a century for this opportunity, but we won't falter. We will continue to raise our voices, share our stories, and demand justice until it is served. For the first time in 100 years, we have a chance, and we won't let it slip away.

Today, as we face the challenges of the world, I urge you to remember that hope is not lost. Cling to it, fiercely, with every fiber of your being. It's easy to be consumed by the darkness, to feel small in the face of adversity. But you are not small. You are powerful, strong, and capable of rising to be your best self. You can find strength in your faith, in your truth, and in the light that shines within you. The world needs that light now more than ever. It needs you. Take a moment to reflect on who you are, what you believe in, and what you stand for. Hold onto hope, stay true to yourself, and never let anyone bury your story. Your voice matters, and your story deserves to be heard. Today, I implore you to be that light, to shine brightly amid the darkness, and to never give up on the hope that lies within you. Don't let them bury our stories.

# 11

# What If?

I knew the journey to Africa would change me in ways I couldn't fully comprehend. As I stood by the Atlantic Ocean, where kidnapped people were once chained and sent off to a life of slavery, I felt a profound sense of grief and anger. The dark history of the transatlantic slave trade was no longer a distant concept I had heard of. Africa was not a faraway place I had dreamt of since I was a little girl, lying in the grass of a cotton field somewhere, looking up at the passing clouds. I was there, finally on the shores of the motherland, where our ancestral journey began.

Africa was far from what I had imagined. It was not just about its natural resources or manpower, but the spiritual energy that permeated the air. The population of Africa was young, with an enormous number of young people. One fact that blew my mind was that Africa was the only continent connected to the Earth's core. Unlike other continents that could be moved around like puzzle pieces, Africa was rooted to the Earth, immovable and unwavering. It symbolized the strength and resilience of the

African people, who had overcome countless challenges throughout history.

I was inspired by seeing Black Africans as presidents and kings who welcomed us "home." Somehow it has made me feel more whole, and sure of my belonging in this life and on this planet. The God I serve did not make us to be slaves. He made us whole and beautiful and put us on rich, vibrant land.

I thought about the other survivors of the attack on Tulsa. How many of them had lived and died without this affirmation of belonging let alone the justice we all deserved? While I was grateful that at more than 100 years old, I made it to Africa and experienced an awakening, I also questioned the injustices and disparities that still existed on the other side of the world, despite the progress we had made. I wondered why we had a justice system and other systems in place if people were still treated unfairly.

Since the Africa trip, my sense of justice has changed. It's grown. I've come to see that when you're blessed, to live to be 109, you still have to give back what you can. Even though it should be something you are born with, justice is not free. Some of us have to work for it, not just for ourselves but for the people we influence. That is a huge part of why my grandson, Ike has been to Ghana several times with our foundation, the Viola Ford Fletcher Foundation. It has also helped me to see the true value of uplifting our communities.

I often fear that the atrocity that befell my community is not the last of its kind. It can happen again. It has taken our generation 100 years to start seeing glimmers of justice, but we must keep holding everyone accountable so that future generations don't have to fight for another 100. It leaves me wondering, what if?

What would have been different if my opportunities had not been stolen?

**What if** I wasn't torn from my prosperous community of "Black Wall Street?" I would have liked to have become a doctor or a registered nurse.

**What if** I didn't have to live a life with Post-Traumatic Stress?" I only know of this because my grandson has PTSD from his service in the military. My family has contributed two men from every generation to the military.

**What if** my employers would have made the proper social security contributions? I wouldn't need to depend on thrift shops and free food services.

**What if** we could have taken more of our valuables that night?

**What if** I could see my childhood friends from that era one more time? I often wonder if they died that night. It's said that the authorities found a "mass grave" in Tulsa recently.

**What if** one of the bodies was that of my neighbor or playmate?

**What if** the massacre never happened, the untold wealth of our people would be amazing." The city would have been seen as a beacon of hope and an example of hard work and entrepreneurship.

**What if** the state and the city didn't opt to turn a blind eye to the violence done to Black people during that time—excusing and dismissing people's murderous behavior? We could have had a Black Wall Street in every city.

**What if** Black soldiers returning from major wars would have been treated with the dignity and respect they earned fighting for the rights of all Americans?

**What if** I could sleep with the lights off, or in a normal bed, or get a full night's sleep without waking up in fear, without thinking I would have to make a hasty retreat?

I carry these questions with me, always lingering in my mind. My grandson tells me it's "therapeutic" to talk about them, and maybe it's time to finally get some things off my chest and tell my damn story! I was asked about the massacre earlier in my life, but I chose not to speak about it. Most of the time, it was White reporters or White journalists who would ask me, or rather, interrogate me. As children, we knew the risks too well. If we ever spoke about it, we could easily be killed.

Just consider that I was only one generation removed from slavery, and Jim Crow was still very much alive. Even in 2022, now as I write this, it's still too painful to revisit. But as for me, Viola Ford Fletcher, God is not done with me yet. I am a living witness to the worst racial massacre in history, and justice is long overdue!

As of writing this book, I have just spent a full year in Tulsa for the first time in almost seventy years. No more running, no more avoiding. It's time to confront the truth and demand justice. No peace can come without justice. We must all face our fears and confront the painful past.

I'd like to share this one piece of wisdom before this book closes:

First, love yourself. Sometimes people, regardless of their color, think less of themselves. They don't know how to manifest positive things in their lives. Being positive is crucial in life, and it starts with loving yourself. The number one thing you need to do is take care of yourself and love yourself. You can't be there for anyone else if you're not true to who you are.

If you're constantly busy trying to please others or fulfill expectations, you end up taking away from yourself. Eventually, it can even compromise your immune system due to a lack of rest and self-care. If you're not rested, you're vulnerable. That's why it's so important to love yourself. You matter.

You matter.

# Epilogue

On this momentous day, May 10, 2023, I am grateful for the blessing of reaching the age of 109. However, instead of joyously celebrating with my loved ones, I find myself within the walls of a Tulsa Courthouse, reliving painful memories of trauma once again.

The scheduling of a hearing on my birthday to potentially dismiss our case feels like another cruel reminder of the hardships I have endured. It is disheartening to think that there is no consideration of this fact, and while it may be coincidental, it deeply affects me. I chose to add this portion of the book after it was complete and about to go to print. I "stopped the presses" because I want my sentiments heard directly, not left to scholarly interpretation. This is how I truly feel.

At the time of this writing, the Judge has requested seven more days to reach a decision, but I wonder if it were to avoid the PR nightmare that dismissing the case on my birthday would have caused.

My greatest desire is to live long enough to witness justice, for someone to acknowledge my profound suffering and the collective pain endured by generations past and those yet to come. The weight of seeking justice for an entire community rests upon my shoulders, and though it is heavy, I carry it with unwavering determination 'til God gives me my last breath, and I finally catch my wings."

# Acknowledgments

We remember and honor those who lost their lives during the Tulsa Race Massacre of 1921 and their descendants. We acknowledge their sacrifice and courage in paving the way for justice and equality. We also extend our deepest condolences to their families and loved ones. May their memories be a blessing and a reminder of our shared humanity.

Special thanks to our amazing lead attorney-at-law, Damario Solomon-Simmons, and his talented wife, Mia Fleming, who is a multi-faceted broadcast talent and book writer.

A heavenly thanks to those who worked behind the scenes to make the world a better place by sponsoring the Viola Ford Fletcher Foundation: Paul Interbitzen of Interbitzen Solutions, Alan Nugent of Palladian Partners LLC, Kristen Raffaelle of Demosophy, St. Simeon Nursing Home, Jamol Pugh, Jeffrey Turenne, and Thomasina Perkins.

We also express our gratitude to the law firm of Schulte Roth & Zabel LLP; President Joe Biden for the private audience given to the family; and Vice President Kamala Harris, who graciously hosted us in her office after the subcommittee testimony on the Hill.

We extend our appreciation to Representative Steve Cohen serving Tennessee's 9th District and the Congressional Black

Caucus, as well as US Congresswoman Sheila Jackson-Lee (D-TX) for her unwavering support.

Our thanks also go to Oklahoma State Representative Regina Goodwin, a descendant of a massacre survivor; James Henri Goodwin, whose family owns the oldest Black newspaper in Oklahoma; The Oklahoma Eagle, Brentom Todd; and Pastors Michael and Natalie Todd; and Pastor Barbara Littlejohn of Transformation Church; and Dr. Tiffany Crutcher, founder of the Terence Crutcher Foundation, named for her twin brother and a board member for Justice for Greenwood.

We also acknowledge the Tulsa Steps Foundation for their assistance in facilitating many blessings throughout the community; and Rev. Dr. Marlin LaVan Har and Rev. Barbara Prose of All Souls Unitarian Church. Special thanks to Michael Thompson chairman and President of Our Black Truth - www.obt.social, title sponsor of "Coming Home: The Journey of a Lifetime" to Accra, Ghana; Ambassador Erieka Bennett, Chief-of-Mission at the Diaspora African Forum in Accra, Rabbi Kohain Nathanyah Halevi, Executive Director PANFESY Foundation, Ghana Tourism Authority; and the beautiful people and government of the Republic of Ghana.

We also appreciate the support of Angela Rye, CEO of IMPACT Strategies; Gayle King, anchor of The CBS Morning Show; Ed Mitzen Business for Good Co-Founder; Tiffany Cross; Roland Martin; DeNeen Brown of The Washington Post; Abby Phillip of CNN; and other concerned news media organizations in the United States and West Africa.

Additional gratitude and acknowledgment to the Oklahoma City Thunder basketball franchise for their contributions to the Black community in Oklahoma.

Special thanks to my first cousin, Frankie Pink, for always standing in the gap for the family; and Teddi Williams, founder of Survivor Stock and a descendant of Black Wall Street survivors; Wess Young, and his wife, Mrs. Cathryn Young.

I also give thanks to Marcus Dwayne Haskin, an author, and friend who started me on this literary journey; Tony Regusters for his dedication and professional guidance; The Tulsa Historical Society and Museum for allowing the use of archival photographs; and Faith Hope Hannah of www.BlackBrownBeautiful.com for her professional guidance.

Mocha Ochoa of Mocha Media Publishing for her understanding of the mere power of the written word of historical black icon Mother Fletcher. She felt it in her spirit that this story had to be told.

Bless my sister, in our mutual fight for justice Lessie Benningfield Randle aka"Mother Randle". Let me not forget my only living sibling, America's favorite Uncle, Hughges Van Ellis aka "Uncle Redd", who worked from "Sunup to SunDown".

# Appendix A: Words to Live By
## MOTHER VIOLA FORD FLETCHER

People often ask me, "Mother Fletcher, what is your secret to a long life!" Well, I truly believe God has allowed me to outlive all my friends and some of my family members to carry the torch for justice. I've taught my grandchildren many things, and I've learned a thing or two from them so here are some words to live by.

"There is no passion to be found playing small--in settling for a life that is less than the one you are capable of living."

Nelson Mandela

"Our greatest happiness does not depend on the condition of life in which chance has placed us, but is always the result of a good conscience, good health, occupation, and freedom in all just pursuits."

Thomas Jefferson

"However, you can never go wrong by treating people, the way you want to be treated."

Anonymous

"Be confident in yourself. "Nobody can make you feel inferior without your permission."

Eleanor Roosevelt

"What's good for the goose is good for the gander is good for the goose!"

Anonymous

"What's done in the dark, will eventually come to light!"

Luke 8:17

"One monkey don't stop the show."

African American Proverb

"Be your best at whatever it is you do best!"

Viola Ford Fletcher

"My mission in life is not merely to survive, but to thrive; and to do so with some passion, some compassion, some humor, and some style."

Maya Angelou

"Each person must live their life as a model for others."

Rosa Parks

"Life's most persistent and urgent question is, 'What are you doing for others?"

Dr. Martin Luther King, Jr.

And one of my favorites:

"Eat Onions with every meal, but don't let them smell your breath and eat clean fruits, don't smoke tobacco, take a shot of spirits and now and again when offered. Control what you can control and don't worry too much about the things out of your control."

Viola Ford Fletcher

# Appendix B: A Chronological List of Known Massacres on Black Americans

Although it is impossible to know the countless horrors perpetrated on individuals of color in this country since chattel slavery, I want to make sure that those before me, whose names have been lost to time, will never be forgotten. Each tragedy and public nuisance listed here must be presented in our schools, passed down through oral history, and addressed in our court systems. We must continue to confront our past until it aligns with the current values projected to the world. Without acknowledgment and abatement of these atrocities, this country will remain broken and divided. I intend to start a foundation that will connect people with the greater good of humanity, not based on skin color, but upon the prosperity of all humans, preserving it for future generations.

I want this foundation to act as a vehicle, transporting us from the realm of possibility to a just and equitable reality. A gathering place where the smartest and brightest come together to embrace modern and green technologies to better people's lives, as well as the planet's. A framework and operating environment for doing the right things for the right reasons because we care about and value our long-term viability as individuals, leaders, and mankind. I'd like to create and give chances that restore optimism and reduce stress.

Before I catch my wings, I've entrusted my grandson, Ike, to fulfill these dreams. Through his diligent work, he will assist people in being healthy, wealthy, and wise. Now I ask you to persevere and progress forward with strength and the Lord's blessing. Stay faithful and dream big while surrounding yourselves with good people who support real success. Please continue this as my life's work. We are greater together than apart. We are one! As my Brother Uncle Redd would say, "One mankind, one humankind." So let's love thy neighbor and be kind. Let's move forward with innovative ideas and green technologies to uplift all mankind.

As we reflect on each city, I ask: Why are the names of Blacks who died in massacres unknown? Why is there only an estimated number of those slaughtered in massacres by White mobs? Why are the survivors still fighting the legal system for these documented wrongs more than 100 years later? Why does it appear that they want us to all die off instead of acknowledging that the lives taken and still affected to this day are of real humans? These are questions I may never have answers to.

Massacres on Black Americans:

- 1863: New York City, New York 1866: New Orleans, Louisiana 1866: Memphis, Tennessee
- 1868: Opelousas, Louisiana
- 1868: Camila, Georgia

- 1868: St. Bernard Parish, Louisiana 1873: Colfax, Louisiana
- 1874: Eufaula, Mississippi
- 1874: Vicksburg, Mississippi
- 1875: Clinton, Mississippi
- 1887: Thibodaux, Louisiana
- 1898: Wilmington, Delaware
- 1906: Atlanta, Georgia
- 1908: Springfield, Illinois
- 1910: Slocum, Texas
- 1917: East St. Louis
- 1919: Washington, DC
- 1919: Chicago, Illinois
- 1919: Elaine, Missouri
- 1920: Ocoee, Florida
- 1921: Tulsa, Oklahoma
- 1923: Rosewood, Florida
- 1943: Detroit, Michigan
- 1985: Philadelphia, Pennsylvania
- 2015: Charleston, South Carolina

Now, at 109 years old, each day I wake up is a gift. My window of time for discovery is short, therefore before I catch my wings, I leave it to you, to find out these answers. I leave it to you to go tell my damn story.

Cover Reveal: Mocha Ochoa, Mocha Media Publishing, Inc.,
Jamol Pugh, 4Black Wall Street.